REBEL PRIEST IN THE TIME OF TYRANTS

Mission to Haiti, Ecuador and Chile

Claude Lacaille

REBEL PRIEST IN THE TIME OF TYRANTS

Mission to Haiti, Ecuador and Chile

translated by Casey Roberts

Baraka Books

Montréal

ISBN 978-1-77186-039-0 pbk; 978-1-77186-050-5 epub; 978-1-77186-051-2 pdf; 978-1-77186-052-9 mobi/kindle

Cover by Folioinfographie
Book design by Folio infographie
Illustrations, back cover, pp 129 and 134 by Hugo Riveros, Santiago, Chile, 1980.

Legal Deposit, 2nd quarter 2015
Bibliothèque et Archives nationales du Québec
Library and Archives Canada

Published by Baraka Books of Montreal.
6977, rue Lacroix
Montréal, Québec H4E 2V4
Telephone: 514 808-8504
info@barakabooks.com
www.barakabooks.com

Printed and bound in Quebec

Société de développement des entreprises culturelles Québec

Baraka Books acknowledges the generous support of its publishing program from the Société de développement des entreprises culturelles du Québec (SODEC), the Government of Quebec, tax credit for book publishing administered by SODEC, and the Canada Council for the Arts.

Canada Council for the Arts

We acknowledge the financial support of the Government of Canada, through the National Translation Program for Book Publishing for our translation activities and through the Canada Book Fund (CBF) for our publishing activities.

Trade Distribution & Returns
Canada and the United States
Independent Publishers Group
1-800-888-4741 (IPG1);
orders@ipgbook.com

Contents

Foreword

Preambular Reflections

Miguel d'Escoto Brockmann, M.M.

Today, as I sit to write this down, is Holy Saturday. That means that tomorrow is Easter Sunday. I like to celebrate Easter every day but tomorrow it will be in a more special way, as with Pope Francis we witness our Church's reconciliation with itself.

I am jotting this down as a sort of preface or, as it occurs to me now, preambular reflections on Father Claude Lacaille's excellent short account of his life as a "disciple of Jesus and a son of the Vatican II" wanting to transmit Jesus' message to those to whom he had been sent in some of the socially, politically and economically most troubled areas in the Latin America of those days.

I am running (or perhaps better said, slowly moving) in my eighty-third year and experiencing the typically assorted kinds of pains and aches compounded by a case of Ménière's disease, it's terrible vertigo episodes and so on. But, like Father Lacaille, I keep going fully enamored with my call to discipleship at a time when the human species, for the first time in its slightly over one-hundred-thousand-year history, is having to face the possibility of its own extinction.

On top of my desk today I see Gustavo Gutierrez' latest book, written with Cardinal Gerhard Ludwig Müller: *On the side of the Poor, the Theology of Liberation*; Edward O. Wilson's latest and perhaps greatest masterpiece: *The Meaning of Human Existence*. On top of that is Michel Chossudovsky's: *The Globalization of War*,

America's 'Long War' against Humanity, an absolutely must-read for all those who mean to live their discipleship of Jesus in today's real and only world. To use very expressive American slang... "*There ain't no other one*." Is this too many books to read at the same time? Perhaps, but none of the multiple and converging anthropogenic crises facing humanity today can be set aside from our minds till we figure out what to do about any single one of them; they must be tackled as a whole.

Those of us, who, like Father Claude and I, were called to be Christian missioners, had our own set of questions to clarify. Besides, missiology was and continues to be one of the branches of theological reflection most ignored for centuries. However, by the time we were "sent" it was becoming more and more clear among missioners that the Holy Spirit had been present and working in every missioner's destination thousands of years before the missioner ever arrived. This was a time of re-discovery that there, in fact, is no god-forsaken place. God's Spirit is, was and will always be everywhere.

The missionary apostolate is therefore a two-way proposition. The missioner first goes to listen, to learn from what the Spirit has already revealed to the people to whom he has been sent. Having done so, the missioner is in a better position to deepen his or her own understanding of the fullness of revelation in Christ, which he has been sent to share. In this manner, both the missioner, him or herself, and the sending community or church, are enriched by the feedback which the missioners send home explaining what he or she have learned from those that he or she were sent to teach.

If we were sons and daughters of Vatican II then, those of us who, like Father Claude and I, were sent to Latin America and the Caribbean to proclaim the good news of Christ, Our Lord, from the 1960s on, are also sons and daughters of Medellin. And Medellin means the Latin American Bishops Conference's enlightened documents on *how* to apply Vatican II, the watershed Council, to the convoluted Latin American reality. It is thus not difficult to imagine the mental disarray and spiritual confusion created by the fact that "disobedience" or rebellion against the teaching authority of a Universal Council of the Church was led precisely by those most responsible for ensuring its implementation. The pontificates of John Paul II and Benedict VXI were primarily committed to undoing Vatican II, to closing the windows that John XXIII had opened to let fresh air in.

I personally think that this situation of living through a papal-led "disobedience" is what explains the widely spread psycho-pathology among the clergy that Eugen Drewermann talks about in his work that is all too important to ignore: *Clergy, Psychogram of an Ideal* (translation in English supposedly by Jeremy Noakes and Leslie Sharp but I don't personally know whether it has been published in English or by whom.)

There are some truths that are extremely painful to accept. But denial is never an adequate solution. Those truths will come back to haunt you and only their acceptance, which is not always synonymous with resignation, will set us free. Fidelity to Vatican II and Medellin led many to risk their lives; they were, in fact, murdered for their obedience to what Popes and Bishops had taught us about what the discipleship of Jesus was all about in our day and age. It is therefore not hard to understand that the turbulence created by witnessing Popes and Bishops shifting their pastoral policies and going against Vatican II and Medellin, would be a very difficult and painful reality to swallow.

The only way to weather the storm created by two successive Pontificates committed to undoing the teachings of Vatican II and Medellin is to reinstall the centrality of Jesus in our souls and lives. We must resist our propensity to put the Church or any Pope in that position, which only Jesus can occupy.

I realize a large number of readers might feel offended by the bluntness with which I have articulated these reflections, and I ask you to forgive me. I mean no offense to anyone, least of all to the alluded popes whom I love and respect very much.

To better understand someone's opinions it serves well to consider where one is coming from. "Consider the source," Aquinas would have said. In my case it is good to remember that I am an old guy. I belong to a generation for which reading Camus' *The Stranger* was still obligatory as part of our university education. His writings in general, but his 1948 statement on what unbelievers expect of Christians presented at the Dominican Monastery of Latour-Maubourg made such a deep impression on me that it still resonates loudly in my heart.

Other writers who have clearly influenced my understanding of what it means to be a follower of Jesus include Romain Rolland whose lights and straight-forwardness in dissertations on things that matter I always admired. In Rolland's biography of Tolstoy, written following the chronological order of appearance of his works, when he comes to *Resurrection* he says that whereas some critics consider *Resurrection* to be the best of his great novels, he, at least, can say that he believes that *Resurrection* is the most sincere and beautiful "poem" ever written in honor of compassion. That, I must say, made me feel great because it is exactly what I feel. Compassion, after all, is what we followers of Jesus must be all about. *Resurrection* also is, besides the best book I ever read, what led me to a deep incursion into everything Tolstoy wrote and into the most important works written about him.

Like many of my contemporaries, among my favorite theologians figure Karl Rahner, Romano Guardini, Karl Adam, Michael Schmaus, Bernhard Häring, Edward Schillebeeckx, Henri Nouwen and all the liberation theologians, at the top of which today I place my dear brother and close friend Leonardo Boff.

The most emblematic persons in my life for what it means to be a follower of Jesus have been: St. Francis, William Lloyd Garrison, Leo Tolstoy, Dorothy Day, Mahatma Gandhi and Martin Luther King, Jr. This explains, I think, why I have never been good at biting my tongue or holding back.

By bringing up the painful past I have only meant to contextualize Father Claude's wonderful testimony before you start walking through its inspired and inspiring pages. Also, I have to admit, I wanted to help those among us who may still not have found out *how* to cope with the 'ripple effect' left by the past spiritual turbulence and storm created by efforts to undo Vatican II and Medellin. After all, it was for upholding the principles stated in their Outcome documents that many of our friends and most admired missioners were murdered, all throughout Latin America and the Caribbean.

And judging from Michel Chossudovsky's latest and quite convincing book, "The storm is not yet over," more and worse is yet to come. The only way to fasten our seat-belts is to hold on fast to Jesus, as that great Christian president, Hugo Chavez of Venezuela, kept telling us to do right up to his lamentably premature death.

With Jesus at the center of our lives we will make it through "America's Long War Against Humanity" or any other lesser ensuing storm, and also work our way out of any lingering aftereffects that past turbulence may have left in our psycho-spiritual make up.

Last night as I began to write down these reflections, I mentioned that it was Holy Saturday. Now is a new day. It is time for rejoicing, for leaving past and painful realities behind us. It is a time for rejoicing because Our Lord has risen in anticipation of what is in store for us. This has to fill our hearts with the enthusiasm needed to effectively keep on proclaiming the Good News of resurrection and salvation.

The Risen Savior has heard his people's pleas and his answer has been wonderful and generous indeed: Francis. Pope Francis, who is the expression of God's loving tenderness to his People, invites us to resume our mission where we left off prior to the papal interruption and tells us in extraordinary simplicity that, "if a Christian is not a revolutionary in today's world reality, he or she is not a Christian."

Francis urges us all to put Jesus, in an unequivocal and noticeable manner, at the very center of our lives. But in so doing, we must keep in mind that Our Lord and Savior was crucified prior to His resurrection. Crucifixion might well be the consequence of our discipleship, as it was for Archbishop Oscar Arnulfo Romero, from whom I received a letter only a few hours prior to his martyrdom. He told me he accepted the invitation to come and stay with me after Easter SUNDAY. Instead, it was I who found myself flying to San Salvador to attend his funeral and concelebrate the mass with all the bishops, where I was placed on the right-hand side of Cardinal Archbishop Ernesto Corripio y Ahumada of Mexico City, the principal concelebrant, as can be seen in photographs of the occasion.

In a few weeks Archbishop Romero will be beatified and I hope to be there again for that occasion as well. That is another demonstration of God's loving tenderness for all of us without exclusions or exceptions for any reason whatsoever.

Our infinitely loving, tender, merciful, compassionate, crucified and forgiving Lord has indeed risen and so will we. Let us rejoice and be profoundly happy as we move forward in our discipleship with Jesus at the center of our lives proclaiming and consolidating the Kingdom of God here on Earth.

Easter Sunday
Managua
April 5 2015

"The day is nearing when people will understand
that Jesus of Nazareth did not mean to
add a new religion to the existing ones,
but, on the contrary, wanted to break down all barriers
that prevent man from being a brother to man
and especially to the most different and despised."
-Ernesto Balducci

1

Ad Limina: On the Threshold

I'm afraid to meet the past
which still returns to haunt my days.
I'm afraid to meet the night,
and the memories of which I dream.
But even someone on the run
must come to stillness now and then
and even if those darkest times
stripped me bare of old conceits,
In secret, I keep my hope alive,
the only thing that's left to me.[1]

El Salvador, September 2008

The plane descended, enveloped by huge white cumulus clouds. Below, fields of sugarcane and corn, pastures, orchards and coffee plantations: a splendid needlepoint of ochers and green. In the *campos* you could see villages and hamlets nestled among the mountains. The tin roofs of the little farmhouses sparkled in the sun. Here and there, the ash spumes of volcanoes punctuated the bucolic countryside of El Salvador, the smallest country in the

1. "Volver," words by Alfredo Le Pera, music by Carlos Gardel; translated by Casey Roberts.

Americas. My face pressed against the window, I thought back on the recent period, the war of 1980. How blood had soaked the earth, spilled during the popular uprising that confronted the oppressive power of a handful of landowning families and an army generously supported by the United States! Blood that seemed to still be flowing down the silty rivers that irrigate the great body of *Mère Terre*, Mother Earth.

In my mind I could hear the voice of the martyred Bishop Oscar Romero, assassinated in 1980 for having defended the victims of this murderous insanity. For more than an hour in his Sunday homily at the cathedral, he enumerated the crimes committed during the week.

> On March 13, in the area of Las Vueltas, the *campesinos* José Aristides Rivera, Orestes Rivera and their mother were murdered. The body of José Efraín Aré valo Cuellas, who had been arrested March 9 in San Miguel, was discovered; it was clear he had been tortured. On the same day, the young men Osmín Landeverde, Manuel Sanchez, Javier Mejía and Carlos García de Quetzaltepeque, were arrested.[2]

The bishop, it seemed, would never stop murmuring this rosary of the horrors experienced by his people.

I thought of Ita Ford, with whom I had worked in Chile, and her partner Carla Piette, both Maryknoll Sisters,[3] who had accepted Bishop Romero's invitation to come to work with refugees of the war in San Salvador. Eight months after the assassination of Romero on December 2, 1980, Ita and three other U.S. missionaries were abducted, raped and murdered by soldiers on the road to the airport, the very road I was rolling down, under a suddenly angry sky.

---

2. Archbishop Romero's homily of March 16, 1980; he would be assassinated on March 24 during the Mass.

3. Maryknoll is the name shared by three organizations that are part of the Roman Catholic Church; the Maryknoll Fathers and Brothers (the Catholic Foreign Mission Society of America), Maryknoll Sisters (Maryknoll Sisters of St. Dominic) and Maryknoll Lay Missionaries.

I started writing this book in this land where, in the name of their faith in a liberating gospel, thousands of peasants, intellectuals, professionals, nuns and priests shed their blood to defend the victims of the war, to oppose murderous policies and a predatory economy, to comfort the afflicted, to breathe courage into a people gasping for air. These women and men remain an inspiration to everyone who still believes that another world is possible.

In the Cathedral of San Salvador, where the prophetic word of Bishop Romero once resounded throughout a Central America in convulsions, calm reigns today. What they worship there is larger than life, other worldly, a religion that serves as a refuge from the social realities that still deeply divide the nation: economic disparities, endemic poverty, violent street gangs, corruption. Archbishop Lacalle exiled the venerated remains of his predecessor Romero to the church's basement, annoyed by the affluence of the crowds of ordinary people who came to pray daily at his tomb. A Church of the Catacombs came into existence, underground, marginalized, banned by the hierarchical authorities. Coming in from the surrounding working-class neighbourhoods, the followers of Archbishop Romero met in the crypt every Sunday and kept their hopes alive, against all odds.

In defense of liberation theology

Oscar Romero was a prophet of the poor throughout Latin America. He was isolated by his fellow bishops, including some who had been integrated into the armed forces as chaplains. The pastor had complained to his closest confidants that Pope John Paul II did not understand him. By condemning liberation theology, the Vatican had turned its back on this ministry of the poor that had been born in the Christian base communities[4] of Latin

4. A group of believing families from a neighbourhood who share their experiences and their faith.

America. In May 2007, Benedict XVI came to Aparecida, Brazil, to inaugurate the Fifth General Conference of the Bishops of Latin America and the Caribbean. At a press conference held during the flight, Pope Ratzinger renewed his accusations. I therefore decided to write to my brother Benedict to respectfully invite him to listen to the believers and set aside his condemnations. The reaction to my letter was enthusiastic and universal: the letter was translated into every European language and posted on the Internet by organizations, parishes and prestigious Christian reviews. I received hundreds of testimonials from Latin America, Canada, Western Europe and even Orthodox dioceses from Moscow and Latvia! I remember this comment left on the web by a Peruvian woman:

> The Latin American that I am understands your life, your authentic path to Jesus, who called you to follow him by putting both feet onto this desiccated ground where problems cease to be theories, transforming themselves into painful truths requiring dialogue with—and love and compassion for—those who suffer. In our land, poverty cannot be ignored, and you've embraced this understanding with your own life… I wish to express to you my deepest admiration and recognition because you, brother, are one of those who have lived their priestly lives in the service of a violated and impoverished people and, even if I don't know you, I'm certain that your face expresses the joy of those who have deeply loved the only Master contemplated by the poor and the disempowered. Thank you for helping me reflect on my life; thank you for having spent yours among us.
>
> Lucrecia

The way that people struggled to survive on this continent bled dry by big capital is what inspired me to write this book, to commit to paper what my eyes have seen. The book is also a plea for the recognition of tens of thousands of missionary sisters, lay people and priests who worked with passion and enthusiasm alongside the oppressed peoples of Latin America and the

Caribbean. Coming from every corner of the globe, they made the aspirations of the people who received them their own.

Open letter to my brother, Benedict XVI

I am writing you this letter because I need to communicate with the pastor of the Catholic Church and there is absolutely no formal communication channel for doing so. I address you as a brother in the faith and in the priesthood, because we have both received the mission of proclaiming the Gospel of Jesus Christ to all nations.

I have been a Québécois missionary priest for forty-five years; I enthusiastically committed myself in the service of the Lord upon the opening of the Second Vatican Council. I have worked among the poor in the hardest-hit communities: the Bolosse neighbourhood in Port-au-Prince under François Duvalier; among the Quichua in Ecuador and finally in the working-class neighbourhoods of Santiago, Chile, during the Pinochet dictatorship.

When I read the Gospel of Jesus Christ at college, the image of the crowds of the sick and the poor that surrounded Jesus made a lasting impression on me, while the numerous seminary priests we studied with at this Catholic college were only interested in talking about sexual morality. I was fifteen.

Liberation theology: an erroneous mix of faith and politics?

On the flight that brought you to Brazil, you once again condemned Liberation theology as a false millenarianism and an erroneous involvement of the Church in politics. I was deeply shocked and hurt by your words. I had read more than once the two instructions on liberation theology that the former Cardinal Ratzinger had published. It describes a red herring that neither represents my experience nor my convictions. I did not need to read Karl Marx to discover the option for the poor.

Liberation theology is not a doctrine or a theory; it is a way of living the Gospel in proximity and solidarity with the excluded and impoverished.

It is indecent to publicly condemn believers who have dedicated their lives—and we are tens of thousands of lay people, priests, religious sisters and brothers from all over the world who have followed the same path. To be a disciple of Jesus is to imitate him, follow him, to act as he acted. I do not understand the persecution and harassment directed against us. Just prior to your trip to Brazil, you silenced Father Jon Sobrino, a committed and devoted theologian, companion of six Salvadorian Jesuit martyrs and of Monsignor Romero, and barred him from teaching in Catholic schools. This man of seventy years served the Church in Latin America with courage and humility through his teaching. Is it heresy to present Jesus as a man and accept the consequences?

During the Pinochet dictatorship in Chile, I was part of a Church valiantly guided by an outstanding pastor, Cardinal Raúl Silva Henríquez. Under his leadership, we walked alongside a people terrorized by fascistic Catholic soldiers who claimed to defend Western Christian civilization by torturing, sequestering, disappearing and killing. During those years, I lived in a poor neighbourhood particularly affected by the repression, La Bandera. It's true, I hid people; true that I helped them flee the country, true that I helped people escape; true that I participated in hunger strikes. I also spent years reading the Bible with people from the poor and working-class neighbourhoods, hundreds of whom discovered the word of God, which enabled them to face oppression with faith and courage, convinced that God accompanied them. I organized community kitchens and crafts cooperatives to enable former political prisoners to regain their place in society. I retrieved murdered bodies from the morgue and gave them a proper human burial. I promoted and defended human rights at the risk of my physical integrity and my life. It's true, the majority of the victims of the dictatorship were Marxists and we had drawn close to them, because these people were our brothers and sisters. And we sang together and prayed together for the end of this ignominy. We dreamed of freedom, together.

What would you have done in my place? For which of these sins do you condemn me, my brother Benedict? What is it about this practice that so troubles you? Is it so far from what Jesus would have done in similar circumstances? How do you think I feel when I hear your repeated condemnations? Like you, I have reached the end of my ministerial service and I expect to be treated with more respect and affection from a pastor. But what you tell me is: "You do not understand the Gospel. This is nothing but Marxism! You are naïve." Isn't there a great deal of arrogance in these pronouncements?

I have just come from Chile where I was reunited in January with seventy of my old friends from the community after a separation of twenty-five years. They received me fraternally, saying:

> "You lived among us, lived like us, you walked beside us during the worst years of our history. You stood with us and you loved us. And that's why we love you so much!"

And they went on to say:

> "We've been abandoned by our Church. The priests have gone back inside their churches; they no longer share with us, no longer live among us."

It's the same in Brazil: over twenty-five years, bishops committed to the landless, the indigenous peoples and the poor from the slums of the big cities have been gradually replaced by conservative bishops who fought against and rejected thousands of base communities where faith was a question of practical reality. This opened an immense vacuum that the evangelical and Pentecostal churches have filled: they remained among the people, and Catholics are moving to these communities in the hundreds of thousands.

Dear Benedict, I beg you to open your mind. You do not have a monopoly on the divine breath; the entire ecclesial community is animated by the spirit of Jesus. I urge you to set aside your convictions; you will soon be judged by the only One allowed to classify us as left or right, and you know as well as I that this judgment will be based on love.

Fraternally,

Claude Lacaille, p.m.é.
Trois-Rivières, May 12, 2007

2
The Gateway to the Path

Trois-Rivières, at the end of the 1950s

At the time, Quebec was governed by the legendary Maurice Duplessis. Nationalism, social conservatism leaning towards fascism, authoritarianism and corruption were the salient characteristics of a Quebec whose people lived in a state of submission blessed with holy water. The Church was a major ally of the provincial leader, who cheerfully kept the churches' parking lots well paved to ensure the votes of all good Catholics. The clergy occupied a preponderant place in society; English Canadians considered Quebec to be a priest-ridden province. Health, education and welfare were the exclusive domains of religious institutions. Closely-knit, we were the descendants of common settlers, French Canadian and Catholic, living on the banks of the St. Lawrence, surrounded by an Anglo-Saxon, Protestant ocean in North America, which for two centuries had done everything in its power to assimilate us and totally control our economy.

I attended the classical colleges at Joliette and Trois-Rivières during my high school years. Our teachers were concerned about our chastity, commented on the encyclicals of austere Pope Pius XII and incited us to take up the priestly vocation. Everything was focused on controlling sexuality. The sixty priests at our college were at our disposal to absolve us of our weekly sinful inclinations. We lived in a totally male environment; the only women present—veiled sisters hidden behind barred windows—worked in the obscurity of the kitchen and the laundry room. We never spoke to them.

I was a religious and curious child: at the age of fifteen, I had read *Le libérateur* by Pierre Thivollier. The book cover showed an angry Jesus, wielding a whip, driving the merchants and money lenders out of the temple. I discovered a Jesus in the service of the poor, the indigent masses, the abandoned, the excluded, whereas in college this social dimension of the Christian message was never spoken of. Why did we pass over in silence the option of Jesus for the poor?

Later, in theology, I had some pretty pitiful and disappointing Bible classes; the focus was on dogma, morals and canon law, all served up in bad Latin and disconnected from reality. I became royally bored. We were cooped up in the seminary, infantilized, without newspapers, no TV, no contact with the outside world, completely cut off from the female half of humanity. This was how we were being prepared to become secular priests in the service of the people!

When I was eighteen, I wore my black cassock all the time, except to go to bed; I was a member of the clergy. "You are gentlemen, not boys," insisted our superior, like a litany. Having been accepted into the clerical caste, we were expected to behave like *petits bourgeois*. Performing more than three hours of daily devotions, my cynical and libertine mind was looking for an outlet. I found one in a Catholic bookstore: a self-teaching *Assimil* Spanish language instruction handbook. I had always enjoyed learning languages. My studies in Latin, Greek and French had given me a solid foundation. I bought the book, covered it with black paper, embellished it with a crucifix made out of band-aids and, equipped with my fake prayer book, began intoning in a deep voice, as if in prayer: *Alberto va a París, Regresará la semana que viene.* I had never heard Spanish spoken, and no one spoke it in Trois-Rivières. Over the summer, the old family shortwave radio, which had been relegated to the basement, became my teacher. I listened to the interminable speeches of Fidel Castro, a powerful speaker, which laid out the foundations of socialism in Cuba and explained clearly and at length the measures taken by the young revolution. Through these broadcasts, I discovered Spanish, political economy and social analysis. I subscribed to *Mensaje*, the magazine of the Chilean Jesuits, which published articles describing the reality of their country and Latin America.

During the fall of 1958, when I entered into my theological studies, we sang the Funeral Mass of the very aristocratic Pius XII at the cathedral. The "Good Pope" John, who succeeded him, raised hopes for renewal. A year later, we sang the same polyphonic mass, this time for the passing of Premier Maurice Duplessis. The light of modernity was finally beginning to dawn in Quebec, providing a crack in the seal of the closed-off seminary. The year of my priestly ordination, 1962, marked the inauguration of the Second Vatican Council. A new era was ushered in by the publication of *The Impertinences of Brother Anonymous*[1] and the unfolding of the Quiet Revolution. We were hungry for a taste of freedom!

I always dreamed of being a missionary

When I was just a little boy, my father took me down to the port of Trois-Rivières after Sunday Mass to watch the ships sailing out to faraway lands. I was totally enthralled when the Sisters of the Immaculate Conception visited my grade school. They were so beautiful, with their blue habits and diaphanous veils!

1. Published in 1960 by the Marist Brother Jean-Paul Desbiens, the small *Les insolences du Frère Untel* (translated as *The Impertinences of Brother Anonymous*) is considered one of the triggers of the Quiet Revolution in Quebec.

They showed black and white slides—this was back in 1946, six years before television came to Quebec—showing African and Chinese children that we could sponsor with twenty-five-cent donations. Later on, missionaries came to our college to tell us about their adventures. I was fascinated by their audacity, literally dreaming about it. Nothing would stop me from becoming a missionary!

In 1961, following the success of the Cuban Revolution, Pope John XXIII, fearing that Catholic Latin America would be submerged under the communist hammer and sickle, invited western churches to send a wave of missionaries to the continent. In missionary magazines, the only publications allowed into our cloistered world, I read about Radio Pius XII in Bolivia. In 1959, the Oblates had begun working in the area of Siglo XX, a large tin mine in the highlands, five thousand metres above sea level. They had started a radio station there to fight communism, since the miners' union was the centre of activities of the Communist Party of Bolivia. People had to choose between the union and the Church. But in 1961, after two years of clashes with the miners, the radio's founder was forced to flee, and there was a change in strategy. The Oblates decided to enter in alliance with the superexploited mineworkers and to make common cause with them. Subsequently, the radio was blown up by the army on five occasions, and the priests were persecuted relentlessly. One day, while two of them were being released after having been placed under arrest, they were roundly rebuked:

"From now on, stick to preaching the Gospel."

And one of them answered: "But that's just what we've always done."

"Yeah well, only talk about what's good in the Gospel."

The option for the poor that the Oblates had adopted made a real impression on me and I wanted to know more about it. During my first trip to South America, it was precisely to Siglo XX that I went on Christmas Day in 1967, and the memory of this visit has stayed with me to this day. This is the missionary that I wanted to become!

During my second year of theological studies, I requested an audience with my bishop to ask that I be sent on mission to Chile. The Monsignor saw red, violently rebuking me. He ended his diatribe by saying that it was a temptation of the devil and dismissed me curtly:

“Kneel down and I will bless you.” “I don’t want your blessing,” I replied, infuriated, and went out, slamming the door.

The Voluntas Dei Institute

Early in the summer, I met Louis-Marie Parent, an Oblate who had just founded a secular institute, the Voluntas Dei. It only took fifteen minutes of conversation for him to accept me: “You’re going to be a missionary. Kneel down and recite the terms of probation.”

I knelt willingly this time. They were enthusiastic years; Father Parent was an apostle of the soul, bold and audacious. During the previous decade, he had sent thousands of young women from Quebec and a multitude of other countries to work in countries all over the globe. We were going to form the male branch of the Oblate Missionaries of Mary Immaculate, and the world opened for us. In a stiff and sclerotic Church, this man inspired me with his spontaneity. He didn’t wait to give me an assignment: “Before going on a mission abroad, you will go to Arthurette, New Brunswick, with Marcel [a colleague who had also recently been ordained]. You’re going to establish a remedial college for young dropouts from classical studies who still want to become priests.”

At twenty-three, I was sent into the middle of the forest, to a small English-speaking mission. Like Nazareth, Arthurette was off the map: a country road with a dozen houses along the Tobique River and a small white wooden *mitaine,* a Protestant meeting house. Our mission consisted of twenty-five Catholic families surrounded by eighteen Protestant churches of every denomination. Potato fields and forests monopolized by the giant Irving oil company filled the landscape.

On mission in the potato fields

The arrival of two young Catholic priests in black cassocks sowed panic in this Protestant Orange Order-dominated community,[2] where there was a fair amount of religious fanaticism on both sides. We were going to train future priests in an old house inherited from a Catholic benefactor. After weathering some insults due to our cassocks, we decided to dress up as Protestant pastors. In black suits and clerical collars, we began visiting our neighbours, a crazy situation, considering my incomprehensible English. But our naïveté and youth made us objects of fun-loving curiosity rather than a threat. The Council had called for ecumenical dialogue; we were going to make it happen. We attended the reformed churches for funerals and to celebrate community holidays. I was struck by the importance given to the Bible in their services, and I was inspired to make scripture study a priority.

In our daily lives, we lived communally with students who had come to brush up in their French, Latin and English, to enable them to continue their studies. In 1964, Father Parent returned from Rome triumphant: he had managed to get permission to open a Theological Seminary in Arthurette, smack dab in the middle of the potato fields. I was responsible for teaching liturgy and that same year, students began to arrive from the Caribbean, Sri Lanka, South Africa, China, the United States, Colombia and later on, a good number of theologians from Haiti, where the Jesuit seminary had been shut down by Duvalier.

2. Orangism comes from Ulster in Northern Ireland, and is an anti-Catholic ideology; it was well established in New Brunswick and opposed to the presence of French-speaking people.

Arthurette was a school of creativity; we were bold and open-minded, with an enviable freedom within the confines of the Edmundston Diocese. A week after my ordination, my first Sunday homily would be offered in little more than rudimentary English: "Pray to the Holy Spirit if you want to understand anything," I told them by way of an introduction.

During these three years, I learned English and discovered the many reform denominations and their commitment to the Bible, and I was also introduced to ecumenism, to dialogue between Christians of various denominations. Received with hostility in the beginning, we learned to approach people without preconceptions and to liberate Catholics from their prejudices. On the death of John XXIII, the four hundred families of the area responded eagerly to our invitation to celebrate an ecumenical funeral. The Good Pope John had been perceived by our Protestant friends as a great Christian, and his openness had touched many hearts.

In the summer of 1965, I was sent to the island paradise of Grenada in the Windward Islands, to accompany a young West Indian colleague recently assigned to the Cathedral of St. Georges. As my stay was scheduled to last for only four months, I proposed to go door to door and talk with people. I discovered a lovely and hospitable people. Little did I know that the Caribbean would be where I would conduct my first mission abroad.

3
A Baptism of Fire in Haiti

Plundered people, people tilled
From top to bottom like earth beneath the plow
People stripped for the enrichment
Of the world's great markets
Let the fire damp fester in your body's secret night
No one any more will dare
Smelt coin or cannon
From the black ore
Of your swelling rage.[1]

Martissant Parish

From Grenada, I arrived in Port-au-Prince on December 18, 1965. My unpredictable superior, Louis-Marie Parent, had invited me to join him to celebrate ten years of Oblate presence in Haiti. Upon my arrival, he asked me to stay for a few months to help out a friend of his, a priest who was painfully recovering from phlebitis. Pierre Alexandre, a Haitian, had been Vicar general of the Diocese of Port-au-Prince since Duvalier's expulsion of the French Archbishop François Poirier in November 1960. He quietly ran this huge diocese from the humble parish of St. Bernadette, in the poor neighbourhood of Martissant.

1. René Dépestre, *Black Ore,* in Ellen Conroy Kennedy, *The Negritude of Poets,* New York, N.Y.: Thunder's Mouth Press, 1989.

I took up residence in the rectory, where I would relearn my theology from a man of God who worked with the disposessed inhabitants of the vast Bolosse slums. Friend of the poor and disempowered, he had practiced his ministry in the hinterland, among the peasantry, travelling the winding paths of the inaccessible mountains on horseback. Sando, to his friends, was a lively and welcoming character, with a huge generosity of spirit and a very open mind; he opposed outright any contact with the regime of François Duvalier.

"In my house we only speak Creole," kindly warned the priest.

I immediately set about learning the language and began practicing Christmas Mass, trying to replace my r's with w's. Accompanied by a group of seminarians, under the open sky in Bois-Verna's Chochote Alley, I celebrated what was probably the most hilarious Eucharist of my career. Siméon, a theology student, was tasked with proclaiming the readings and preaching. At the moment when I invited the faithful to "lift up our hearts," I mixed up the word "heart" with the word "prick," two very similar words in Creole. A tsunami of laughter erupted and continued throughout the celebration, and the story spread around the entire country ... and is still told to this very day.

During the day, I'd pass the hours with two orange vendors who conducted business on the steps of the church. "*M-vini lékol,*"[2] I'd say to them, and we'd chat happily for quite a while, sitting on some *twipot tichèz.*[3] The ladies were very glad to be able to teach this young white man who was eager to learn from them. I discovered that the language of a people is the key to understanding their thoughts and feelings. Creole is a language full of images and proverbs, peppered with bursts of humour and music. The intonations and gestures that accompany speech highlight its nuances, outbursts of laughter give it its rhythm. In

2. Creole for "I'm coming to school" (*je m'en viens à l'école*).
3. Creole for "Chairs to sit and chat on" (*chaises pour papoter*).

the courtyards of people's homes, at the market, on the street, along the hillside trails people stopped to chat; these exchanges are called *odians*,[4] or "small talk." It is amusing to note that the Creole phrase *palé fwansé* (*parler français*—"to speak in French") means ironically "talking without saying anything."

Pierre Alexandre was in the avant-garde in applying the liturgical reforms of Vatican II. The Eucharist was now celebrated in Creole, to the delight of the people. On Sunday mornings, Sando held Mass at four o'clock, to which flowed a tightly-packed crowd of the poorest people: street vendors, shopkeepers, craftsmen, servants, *restavèk*,[5] and others. This Mass had originally been instituted so that the slaves could drape their nakedness under the cloak of darkness, but still be able to resume their tasks at dawn, as the labour code at the time of slavery allowed for fourteen hours of labour per day. Some employers in business today seem not to know that slavery was officially abolished in 1794!

At Sainte-Bernadette, the four o'clock Mass was the most popular, a real celebration. For two hours, Villeroi, perched on a bench, energized the meeting with his accordion, sometimes accompanied by mesmerizing drums. The pews were packed, the aisles and the choir were swarming with people. The people sang and shouted at the top of their lungs the prayers and refrains they all knew perfectly by heart. It was evocative of an oppressed people—thirsty for freedom—shouting its suffering to God.

During Holy Week, we sang the Passion of Christ in Creole. The faithful were moved; their tears, shouts, and outbursts resounded in the church as if it were an actual funeral. The community understood, for the first time in five hundred years

4. Creole for audience.

5. Creole for the standard French: *reste avec* (stay with). Children placed by their biological families with both urban and rural families. The children are expected to perform domestic tasks, often in conditions akin to slavery, in exchange for their care.

of Christian teaching, the terrible story of the assassination of Jesus by the authorities. The Haitian people had always heard the narrative in French, but in their own language they could finally identify with Jesus as a victim of repression. I'd always had the desire to deepen my understanding of the Bible and was carried away by my parishioners' uninhibited thirst to learn. But I was left with a fundamental question: how can these ancient texts be made accessible and useful in today's world, when they seem so difficult to interpret?

I would occasionally take the time to observe the men and women who came to pray in the church during the day. A street vendor had set her heavy basket down in front of a statue of the Virgin, and stood upright, hands raised to the sky. She prayed aloud, speaking of her misfortunes, her violent spouse, her child's hunger, the money she didn't have. She insisted on being heard, begging and crying at the same time. I was upset; how could you remain indifferent to such an outpouring? Another time, I heard the prayer of a man who stood at the door of the Church of St. Joseph, patron of the workers. He was furious at the saint for not listening to his prayers and for not helping him to find a job. He cursed angrily as he would have at a co-worker, protesting how his misery was unbearable. The empty nave bounced the echo of his lament all the way to heaven. It was not how I had learned to pray at the seminary, but I must admit that if I had been St. Joseph, it would have moved me to the bottom of my heart.

During the week, after five o'clock Mass in a packed church, the ladies of the Légion de Marie invited me to go with them to visit the sick. In a crisp white cassock, I walked the pathways that wound through squalid makeshift huts. Clinging to the mountainside, the neighbourhood had neither sewerage services nor running water, and during heavy rains, flooding caused chaos. I was sick to my stomach to see such deprivation. I will never forget the morning when I crawled into a one-by-two-metre cardboard hut on all fours, where a young mother was dying from terminal cancer. Without care or medicine, her life flowed out of her onto the tamped earthen floor, while her two hungry little children crawled over her, naked. I was shocked and disgusted that I only had a powerless prayer and some useless anointing oil to offer her. The neighbours kindly thanked me and reassured me they were going to take the little ones in … as if there could have been any doubt!

I've never forgotten it! I bawled all day long in my room, like a bleating calf, shook to my very essence. I could never have imagined any situation so unjust and demeaning. A middle-class Quebecker, raised in comfort, I was ashamed to be part of a world that ignores the fact that such realities exist. I wanted to take up arms to fight against those responsible for this violent injustice and I felt a horrible powerlessness, because I was in no way prepared to understand the situation in Haiti, to analyse what was going on. I was experiencing my deepest crisis of faith.

"People are starving to death and I'm singing Masses!"

Usually in a good mood, Villeroi the accordionist came to me one day, in despair. There had been a terrible tragedy: his wife had just given birth to twins!

He was crying:

> "What am I going to do? You know, I've already thrown four children into poverty, and now I've got two more coming. These little innocents will be hungry every day of their existence, just like I've been. You can't understand, Father, you've never been hungry! Me, since the day I was born, I've had a twisting cramp in my guts, as if my large intestine is about to swallow the small one. I had to hock my tools to pay the doctor. I'm finished."

I consider those years as my missionary training, and Haiti as the place of my baptism, a baptism of fire. Sando embraced me like a son and graced me with his friendship and trust. He taught me about the world of the poor through his stark, compassionate and open-minded testimony. He was a prophet to the disempowered that he loved so deeply. Through Sando, I discovered this extraordinary people who changed me and made me the man I've become. The cry heard every day in Haiti: *mwen gwangou*, I'm hungry, still pierces my heart, after fifty years! This specter haunts the abandoned masses of the Pearl of the Antilles to the present day, both in the city and in the country.

Fourth Avenue in Bolosse

In addition to the parish ministry, my presence in Haiti included a very specific mission: I was responsible for setting up the Voluntas Dei Institute. In 1964, Duvalier had closed the large seminary in Port-au-Prince, and candidates for the priesthood continued to be under house arrest with their families. My supervisor, Louis-Marie Parent, surprisingly managed to land an interview with Papa Doc; he asked to be allowed to bring some young theologians to Canada to complete their studies.

"But what gives you the right do you ask me that?" pointedly asked the dictator.

Parent quickly stood up, walked around the large desk of Duvalier, who recoiled. He took his hand and said with pathos: "On behalf of the friendship between our two peoples!"

Permission was immediately granted.

A few months later, a large contingent of Haitian students arrived in Trois-Rivières, happy to be able to resume their studies. I stayed in Haiti to welcome them upon their return and to establish the new institute. A year later, I was joined by Eddy Julien, who would become like a brother to me, and my friend Léo Deshaies, a simple nurse as he defined himself. With the financial support of the Oblates, we bought a property on Fourth Avenue in Bolosse and began to accept students interested in joining the Voluntas Dei Institute as lay people or future priests. The house had room for a dozen students and academics.

The alliance between the dictator and the altar

By the time the young Haitian priests began to return from Canada, the situation of the Catholic Church had changed in Haiti. Duvalier had secured the appointments of five new Haitian bishops from the Vatican. The concordat between the Government of Haiti and the Vatican stipulated that priests and bishops were to be appointed by the president of the country. Papa Doc had long wanted to have a Haitian clergy that was loyal and submissive.

In 1960, Duvalier brutally expelled François Poirier, the French Archbishop, from Port-au-Prince. A few months later, Poirier's Haitian auxiliary Rémy Augustin, was also expelled. In 1962, Duvalier expelled the Bishop of Gonaïves, the Breton Jean-Marie Paul Robert, who had forbidden his priests to recite the prayer prescribed at the end of the Mass for the President of the Republic. Twelve French priests were expelled in 1963 and the following year, eighteen Canadian Jesuits who ran the capital's major seminary were also thrown out.

During diplomatic negotiations over the appointment of the bishops, a petition was sent to Rome through Louis-Marie Parent. A group of Haitian priests demanded guarantees that future pastors would not be regime straw men. Nothing came of it: five bishops were consecrated in the cathedral of the capital by the Papal Legate Antonio Samoré, on October 28, 1966. Duvalier was seated in the choir with the clergy, flanked by his armed Tonton Macoutes.[6] The bishops' residences were once again furnished and restored at the expense of the state, an air-conditioned luxury vehicle given to each of the new prelates. The alliance between the palace and the altar was sealed. Duvalier proclaimed himself the "spiritual father

6. The tonton macoute, the equivalent of the bogeyman, snatches children and puts them in his bag (macoute) at night. This was the name given by the people to the president's bodyguards, whom the regime had pompously called "National Security Volunteers."

of the nation," "the energizer of souls," "the apostle of the public good," and he solemnly distributed to "his" clergy the "breviary" of the revolution (that he wrote himself), an invitation that Sando and I declined by leaving the capital that very day.

Initially, the Haitian clergy were happy with the new situation. Indeed, it was high time that the Catholic Church adopted a native clergy. The missionaries from Brittany, dedicated and hardened men, appeared to have had little interest in promoting Haitians: only a quarter of the clergy were Haitian citizens when Papa Doc took power in 1957. The new archbishop of the capital, François-Wolf Ligondé, returned from Europe where he had been trained during the period of the Council. At first he surrounded himself with progressive priests, but the honeymoon was short-lived: little by little, it was observed that the bishops were blatantly submissive to the dictates of the national palace, which bought their silence and skillfully turned them into accomplices.

Caught up in this whirlwind of events, I had little sway with the Episcopal Conference. I was just a young foreigner, twenty-six, and the bishops were desperate to rein in the Haitian priests just returned from Canada, who were hoping to work in small teams in the countryside as proposed by the Institute, instead of the usual practice of having young priests serve as assistants to parish priests who were often authoritarian, conservative and anti-reform.

My friends in the Haitian clergy would soon find themselves persecuted in turn. In April 1969, the dictator put sweeping anti-communist measures into force. Thirty young members of the Communist Party of Haiti, detained in Fort-Dimanche, were executed in the public square in the presence of students and functionaries, in a calculated scene of terror. The purpose of the campaign was to win the support of the Americans and to regain access to economic aid suspended during the Kennedy administration. On May 25, the day of the Pentecost, Archbishop Ligondé publicly supported the dictator in his homily.

Until then, I had thought the Church holy, but I was shocked by the compromises made by the scheming and cowardly hierarchy. Outraged, I confronted Ligondé. Not having studied at the Pontifical Academy of Noble Ecclesiastics, I did not use any diplomatic language. I sharply expressed my disgust and my disagreement. Annoyed by my impertinence, the "Monsignor" took steps to ensure my departure; it was clear I had become a "communist." On June 3, I left Haiti, my heart broken and in full rebellion.

The conflict with the archbishop grew louder by the day, until August 15, when the priests of Saint-Martial college were kidnapped and forcibly brought to the presidential palace. The archbishop handed them their passports, and they were led under armed escort to the airport for deportation. They arrived in Paris destitute and penniless. All were Haitians, but there were no protests from the bishops and that same day, Ligondé and Minister of Religious Affairs Chalmers presented the new superior of the seminary to Tontons Macoutes standing at attention! *Le Nouveau Monde* headlined: "Communism, the enemy. Deportation of nine Catholic priests guilty of Marxist activities." In October, I wrote in *Le Devoir* of Montreal, under the pseudonym "*Un Canadien errant*":

> In Haiti, the poor feel betrayed by the so-called official Church and the people are sadly disappointed to have church leaders more attentive to politics than to pastoral work. Fear is eating away at a hierarchy that avoids any clear definition of the problems. Committed laymen and priests are being neutralized; any apostolic work with youth and the destitute masses is suspected of being communist.

Before dying in 1971, Papa Doc installed his son, Jean-Claude, as president for life. A Thanksgiving ceremony was held at the cathedral. Archbishop Ligondé, clasping Jean-Claude's hand, gave this astonishing speech:

> Your authority is a participation in the Divine Authority. As Head of State, you are not a mere delegate of the community, Excellency, but

His guide in the pursuit of His highest goals. For the first time since the glorious days of our independence, power is given to youth.

The reign of terror

It was my plan to tell you how I came to Haiti as an ingenuous young missionary, imbued with religious ideology to save the world. I had no idea what was going on in Haiti, except that it was ruled by an evil dictator. When I arrived, I was warned to never talk about politics. People whispered to one another and looked around before discussing current events. Fear paralysed everyone. Sando warned me to be cautious with certain Duvalierist priests.

One day a soldier was directing the chaotic traffic on the main street, opposite the rectory. He intercepted a jeep driven at high speed by a powerful Tonton Macoute. Offended, the guy got out of his vehicle and administered a humiliating public beating to the uniformed soldier. Nicknamed Ti-Bobo, the proud bully was in the habit of terrorizing storekeepers and street vendors, extorting money from their meager incomes. That night, the enraged soldier appeared at the home of his attacker and demanded he come out: when Ti-Bobo opened the door, he was riddled with bullets. The people danced late into the night around his corpse. The soldier was executed.

The dictatorship of François Duvalier, 1957-1971

A physician, François Duvalier rose to prominence in the hinterland as a director of the campaign against yaws[7] funded by the United States, which led to him becoming, until 1950, Minister of Health. When the Estimé government fell to a military coup, Duvalier, in opposition, was forced underground. After the subsequent fall of

7. Yaws is a tropical disease found under extreme poverty conditions, caused by bacteria and affecting the skin.

General Magloire, Duvalier became a candidate for the presidency, and on September 22, 1957, assumed power with the support of the generals who believed he would be easily manipulated. This previously discreet and unthreatening man went on to monopolize power, subjugating the army and the Catholic Church and playing cat and mouse with the American Embassy in pursuit of his goals.

Eighty-seven percent of the Haitian social pyramid was then composed of peasants and urban and rural poor, while eleven percent of the population belonged to a middle class comprised of functionaries, employees, professionals and artisans. During the reign of Papa Doc, more than ten thousand intellectuals fled the country; in Canada alone, there were two hundred and fifty Haitian doctors in 1969. The big bourgeoisie that controlled the country accounted for just one and a half percent of the population: merchants, industrialists, large landowners, government officials and army officers.

Admirer of Jean-Jacques Dessalines, Duvalier appropriated the slogan of the national hero, "*Koupé tèt, boulé kay*."[8] To prevent the army from overthrowing his government, he surrounded himself with a Presidential Guard of five hundred soldiers and a militia of eight thousand Tonton Macoutes recruited primarily from the poorest strata. The Macoutes enjoyed complete impunity and lived off the proceeds of criminal acts and extortion; they formed a state-sanctioned mafia. More than half of the meager national budget of twenty-eight million dollars was allocated to the president's security.

During his fifteen years in power, Papa Doc successively eliminated his most trusted aides, either by sending them abroad as ambassadors or by simply shooting them. In 1967, his advisors convinced him that the opposition was preparing a plot against his life from outside the country, and seven senior members of

8. Creole for the French: *Coupez les têtes, brûlez les maisons.* (Cut off their heads, burn down their houses).

the Presidential Guard were implicated. In all, nineteen army officers, accused of conspiracy, were tried and sentenced to death. On June 8, Duvalier personally commanded the firing squad and carefully selected the men who would fire on these "traitors in khaki." Each of the chosen officers had to shoot a person with whom he had significant ties. Max Dominique, his son-in-law, was part of the squad. Militiamen were stationed on rooftops, machine guns trained on the firing squad to protect Papa Doc from treason. Max Dominique was then stripped of his military status and named ambassador to Paris with his wife, Marie-Denise Duvalier: the presidential couple kindly accompanied them to the airport.

In alliance with the oppressed

Immersed in a world of terror for four years, I was paralysed by a general feeling of helplessness. I wondered if the religion that I represented, even considering the Vatican Council reforms that were taking place around us, had only served to numb the intolerable suffering experienced by an entire people. God knows the people of Haiti draw their strength from their religious faith! But the Catholic hierarchy had sold their souls to the devil, and for me, it constituted a terrible betrayal. It had become personally unbearable to stay silent, and, more importantly, to accept my powerlessness to change things. But what could I do? I was consumed with indignation, and I'm convinced I would have taken up armed struggle if the opportunity had been given to me. I returned to Quebec sick, weakened by a case of typhoid that twisted my guts and made me bleed profusely. However, I no longer felt at home in my native Quebec; something had definitely changed in my life. The Haitian experience had turned me upside-down and shook me from head to toe. What I saw and heard in the midst of the Haitian people is forever etched in my memory. I discovered a people with superhuman vitality; I heard their cries and witnessed their oppression, and was shocked by the betrayal of my Church. I experienced great friendships, a warm relationship with the people from the poor neighbourhoods and with the students who shared my life in the house in Bolosse. They had even jokingly designated me *nèg po lanvè,* [9] a compliment that made me blush with pride.

This ethical indignation would enrich both my spirituality and my reading of the Gospel.

Since then, I have never ceased to be a rebel, viscerally and spiritually, like Pierre Thivollier's notion of Christ the Liberator casting out the merchants from the temple. I dived into the subversive message of Jesus of Nazareth and promised myself that until my last breath, my covenant would be sealed with the oppressed, the marginalized, the impoverished of the world.

---

9. Creole: "*Nègre avec la peau à l'envers*" (Negro with his skin inside-out).

Studying theology at the Grand séminaire de Trois-Rivières in 1959. We were virtually sequestered, cut off from the world.

The year of my ordination, 1962, marked the inauguration of the Second Vatican Council. We entered into a new era that gave us wings. We were hungry for freedom.

A visit to the village of Chauffard where the Breton missionary Father Royan (centre) and Oblate Nina Joseph (right) lived.

The Haitian capital Port-au-Prince was surrounded by large crowded neighbourhoods where poverty was a fact of life.

François Duvalier, aka Papa Doc, terrorized the Haitian people for fifteen years. Half of the country's meagre national budget was spent on the president's own security.

Pierre Alexandre (centre) welcomed me like a son and graced me with his friendship. Eddy Julien (right) became a true brother.

A typical street in Latacunga in the Ecuadorian Andes.

Celebrating Holy Week with two Quichua rural community leaders.

4
Latin America: The Backyard of the United States

When the trumpet sounded, it was
all prepared on the earth,
and Jehovah parceled out the earth
to Coca-Cola, Inc., Anaconda,
Ford Motors, and other entities:
The Fruit Company, Inc.
reserved for itself the most succulent,
the central coast of my own land,
the delicate waist of America.[1]

Before continuing the story of my two subsequent missions in Ecuador and Chile, I would like to take a moment to consider the political and social situation prevailing at that time in what was then called the United States' backyard, the Caribbean and Latin America.

1. Pablo Neruda's epic poem "The United Fruit Company" from *Canto General* is translated by one of America's foremost poets, Robert Bly in Robert Bly, John Knoepfle and James Arlington Wright, *Neruda and Vallejo*. Beacon Press, Boston, Mass., 1993

Colonized peoples want emancipation

The decade of the 1960s was a time of great turmoil around the world. African countries colonized by Europe gained their independence. From 1960 to 1970, twenty-eight new countries joined the United Nations. A thirst for emancipation and freedom swept the world.

The Cold War was raging: the United States and the Soviet Union competed for world domination. The aggression of the U.S. Army in Vietnam continued from 1961 until 1975; to rationalize this terrible war they claimed to be halting the spread of communism. It was a protracted imperialist war; dirty, unpopular, culminating in a humiliating defeat for the U.S. Organized and disciplined peasants had overcome the most powerful army in the world. The result: one million Vietnamese soldiers and four million civilians were killed; 8,774,000 Americans soldiers participated in the carnage.

During the same period, the United States was confronted with a socialist revolution one hundred and seventy kilometres off the coast of Florida, on the island of Cuba; U.S. businesses were nationalized and land owned by United Fruit Company was expropriated. The invasion of the island, planned by Eisenhower and commanded by Kennedy at the beginning of his term in 1961, was a total failure. The Cuban people stood with the revolution and won a decisive victory over the Americans at the Bay of Pigs. As a result of the embargo imposed by the United States, Cuba, isolated from Latin America, drew closer to the Soviet Union, which bartered oil for sugar cane. In October 1962, the Soviets installed nuclear missiles on the island, pointed at the United States. The crisis nearly evolved into a nuclear confrontation between the two superpowers. But ultimately, tragedy was avoided: the Soviets withdrew their missiles in exchange for a written promise from Kennedy not to attack the government of Fidel Castro. This marked the beginning of "détente" or "peaceful coexistence."

Internally, the United States was confronted by the movement for the emancipation of the African-American people. After the abolition of slavery, African Americans had continued to be beaten, lynched, attacked, and marginalized in American society. The abolition of segregation was legally adopted in 1954; whereas in 1965, over seventy-five percent of Southern schools were still segregated. In the early 1960s, blacks in the South rebelled. At the end of the decade, they rose up in insurrection in hundreds of Northern cities. In 1965, there were the "long, hot summers," when the anger of the excluded exploded into social violence. Malcolm X, a leader of the Nation of Islam, was assassinated. The Baptist minister Martin Luther King led a broad liberation movement, inspired by Gandhi and the idea of active non-violence. In 1967, a year before his assassination, he broke his silence and joined the movement against the Vietnam War. "From Vietnam to South Africa to Latin America, the United States is on the wrong side of a world revolution,"[2] he said. Alongside other Christian groups, King launched the Poor People's Campaign, a second stage in the fight for civil rights, with the goal of eradicating poverty. "It must not be just black people," he said. "We must include American Indians, Puerto Ricans, Mexicans, and even poor whites."[3]

The apostle of the civil rights movement was assassinated in 1968.

The revolution of the "bearded ones" in Havana brought about a change in U.S. foreign policy towards Latin America. John F. Kennedy and his advisers devised a plan for intervention in the region called the Alliance for Progress, with twenty

2. Speech by Martin Luther King in New York, April 4, 1967: "Beyond Vietnam: the time to break the silence." Krenn, Michael L. (1998). *The African American Voice in U.S. Foreign Policy Since World War II*. Taylor & Francis. p. 29.

3. Speech by Rev. Martin Luther King announcing the Poor People's Campaign, Dec. 4, 1967.

billion dollars earmarked for economic development and massive military assistance. The decade of the sixties was marked by the emergence of a new generation of Latin American armies and by the transfer of dollars and hardware from the United States military to Latin America. Designed by the Pentagon and the CIA to halt the advance of socialism, the School of the Americas, run by the United States Army, provided training for Latin American dictators and their armed forces. Torture was systematically taught, with the collaboration of experienced operatives from Israel and South Africa. Brazil became the first military dictatorship in 1964; thereafter, the Brazilian military helped to train the repressive forces of its neighbouring countries. This new generation of armed forces eventually seized power all over the continent, establishing dictatorships that set about crushing any vestige of social progress during the 1970s, particularly in Uruguay, Chile and Argentina.

Everything seemed possible

The victory of the Cuban revolution on January 1, 1959 sent torrents of hope cascading among the impoverished masses of Latin America, and young people proudly wore the red-star-topped beret of Ernesto Che Guevara. A revolutionary groundswell surged across Latin America: the Montoneros in Argentina; the MIR (Revolutionary Left Movement) in Chile and Bolivia; the Tupamaros in Uruguay; in Colombia, the ELN (National Liberation Army), with the emblematic image of the guerrilla priest Camilo Torres, and the Revolutionary Armed Forces of Colombia; not to mention the Sandinista Front in Nicaragua; the Farabundo Martí National Liberation Front in El Salvador; the EGP (Guerrilla Army of the Poor) and the ORPA (Revolutionary Organization of Armed People) in Guatemala, and so on.

In the context of the Cold War, the Soviet Union resolutely abstained from promoting a revolutionary process in the "backyard of imperialism." The alliance with Fidel Castro was not constituted until after the consolidation of the revolution. For strategic reasons, the Moscow-oriented communist parties of the region generally opposed the revolutionary groups in the field. But Latin America was in complete turmoil and ready to take on U.S. imperialism. Soviet dogma could not prevent the revolution from spreading, and the Cuban revolution opened new perspectives.

This was the social and political climate that greeted me as I began my work in South America.

5
I am the Son of Vatican II

Let's open the windows of the Church
and let in some fresh air.

John XXIII

The announcement of the Ecumenical Council by Pope John XXIII in January 1959 lit a ray of hope in the Catholic Church. The "Good Pope" invited us to open the windows and doors to let the fresh air of new perspectives into this Church that resembled more and more a conservatory of the past. The believers of my generation rode the wave of the formidable dynamic triggered by this extraordinary meeting of two thousand five hundred of the world's bishops at the Vatican. Over three years, meeting four times for sessions of two months, the pastors of the Catholic Church and guests from other Christian churches reflected and attempted to reform this two-millennia-old institution with a sense of freedom and creativity,

The Catholic Church was changing. The social teachings and encyclicals of John XXIII and Paul VI had encouraged the emergence of a social Christianity that prioritized social justice and the defense of the working class. These ideas had made their way to Europe and were put into practice by various Catholic Action movements—which advocated the evangelization of the city by the laity[1]—and also by the movement of worker priests. Christian Democratic political parties, which sought to humanize capitalism, were also a byproduct of papal encyclicals. In 1965, the Vatican Council promulgated a magisterial document advocating dialogue between the Church and the contemporary world.

> The joys and the hopes, the griefs and the anxieties of the men of this age, especially those who are poor or in any way afflicted, these are the joys and hopes, the griefs and anxieties of the followers of Christ. Indeed, nothing genuinely human fails to raise an echo in their hearts.[2]

Returning from the Council where they had been relatively discreet, the Latin American bishops met in plenary session in Medellin in 1968. They found that throughout Christian Latin America, conditions of poverty and social injustice reigned. The Catholic hierarchy, which had historically lined up on the side of the families of conservative large landowners, announced a change in perspective with the preferential option for the poor as a testimony to the Gospel of Jesus. They would now promote the emergence of Christian base communities situated among the poor and whose social justice actions would be inspired by a reading of the Bible from the people's perspective.

The fight for justice

The 1971 Synod of Bishops in Rome published the document *Justice in the World*, rejecting the idea that poverty would disappear simply through economic development. The bishops considered action for justice as a constitutive dimension of the

1. Laity here means "the faithful," that is to say, believers who are not part of the clergy.
2. Vatican II, Pastoral Constitution *Gaudium et Spes* on the Church in the Modern World, 1965, No. 1.

preaching of the Gospel.[3] The Church should also practice justice in its own house, insisting that women be given their rightful place. "We also urge," the bishops wrote, "that women should have their own share of responsibility and participation in the community life of society and likewise of the Church."[4] That same year, the Peruvian theologian Gustavo Gutiérrez published his book *Liberation Theology*,[5] which developed the idea of an evangelic spirituality centered on the liberation of the poor. I had the privilege of hearing Gustavo in Montreal in 1969, upon my return from Haiti. His remarks greatly inspired me and helped me to find the path I was ultimately to take. I had finally found a theology that could illuminate and guide my experience. Where previously I had been constrained by my powerlessness in the face of the social evils that surrounded me, I now began to see that I could be an agent of change by exercising my calling as a missionary.

The Bible unlocked

One of the principal achievements of Vatican II was to give the Bible back to the faithful. During the Reformation in the sixteenth century, taking advantage of the invention of printing, Luther translated the biblical text into German in order to make it accessible to people. But Rome chose to keep the Bible in Latin, captive in the hands of the clergy. With Vatican II, the Roman Catholic Church could finally speak in the vernacular. The Bible came out of the closet. Believers could now drink freely at the source of their faith and spirituality.

I enthusiastically committed myself to sharing the richness of the Bible with the people of Haiti, Ecuador and Chile. I dived into

---

3. Synod of Bishops, *Justice in the World,* Rome, 1971, No. 6.
4. *Ibid.*, No. 42.
5. Originally published in Lima, Peru in 1971 as *Teologia de la liberación,* and in English as *A Theology of Liberation,* Maryknoll, New York, 1973. The book has been translated into twenty languages.

the ancient texts as a way to understand what was actually happening in the world, and in the midst of the people, I learned how to re-read this revolutionary book. The poor and the oppressed taught me to enter into the Gospel in the light of their reality. Together, we found the inspiration to continue to live fully, to seek justice and to build a world of peace and fraternity.

The Church, People of God in solidarity with all humanity

Another achievement of the Council was the redefinition of the Church as the People of God, a doctrine which was articulated in the three major Conferences of Latin American Bishops in Medellin (1968), Puebla (1979) and Santo Domingo (1992). Synods, chapters and numerous meetings of all kinds were held in local Churches to root themselves in the reality of the poor. The bishops took courageous positions, based on the concrete conditions existing in each country. Many movements of priests were initiated, demanding to be heard and speaking out on topics related to their ministry. A historic decentralization of the great institution of authoritarian Christianity directed from Rome was taking place: Churches emerged among the people that were deeply rooted in their social and cultural realities. We were experiencing the democratization of the grassroots in an enthusiastic atmosphere.

Above all, this dynamism appeared in the base communities, supported by the Conference of Latin American in 1979: "The Church's commitment to the poor and the oppressed and the emergence of base communities have helped the Church to discover the evangelizing potential of the poor."[6]

The base communities bubbled up like fresh water springs, as we began to share the word of God with people in their neighbourhoods, homes and in the countryside. In every country

6. Puebla Document, No. 1147.

and in different contexts, on the occasion of religious festivals, novenas and other devotions, people gathered to read the Bible, discuss their problems and look for solutions to the challenges of their collective lives in a climate of faith and prayer. These small groups, with democratically elected leaders, multiplied among the workers, the indigenous peoples, the peasantry, in the poor neighbourhoods. The emergence of military dictatorships that proliferated like weeds during those years led to the base communities becoming refuges of freedom of expression and they formed centres of resistance to oppression. The God of Exodus who sees the oppression of the slaves and comes down to free them inspired the struggles of trade unionists, women, the homeless, the landless, the unemployed and impoverished.

Solidarity is the tenderness of the peoples[7]

The Council document *Gaudium et Spes* specified that the Church must be involved in the world and in constant dialogue with society. "This community [of Christians] realizes that it is truly linked with mankind and its history by the deepest of bonds."[8]

I offer as an example, with great affection, the story told by Leónidas Proaño, the Bishop of Riobamba, Ecuador. Arriving in his diocese in 1954, he was faced with two major challenges: first, the humiliating and marginal situation of the Quichua peasants who constituted the majority of the population and second, the construction of a great cathedral promoted by the local bourgeoisie. The pastor hastened to explain to his people that his priority was the construction of a church formed by indigenous brothers and sisters, a church of living stones. The cathedral could wait! For thirty-one years Proaño devoted himself to the development and liberation of the Quichua communities, inces-

7. Gioconda Belli, Nicaraguan poet.

8. *Gaudium et Spes*, no. 1.

santly persecuted by the ruling class, his fellow bishops and the Papal Nuncio.

Guided by pastors who were also prophets of the God of life, all over Latin America, the solidarity of the base communities with the poor led to the martyrdom of thousands of Christian women and men, who were persecuted and vilified like the biblical prophets.

The masters of the law impose their sacred power

In 1969, following a tour of twenty countries in Latin America, Nelson Rockefeller warned against the subversive ideas finding expression in the Latin American Catholic Church. "Currently, the Church [...] with its profound idealism is vulnerable to subversive penetration; and ready to undertake a revolution if necessary to end injustice."[9] Pope John Paul II journeyed to Puebla, Mexico, in 1979, to address the Conference of Latin American Bishops, marking his intention to rein in liberation theology and to bring any activity in the social sphere under the control of Rome. The Pope, who had contributed greatly to the fall of the communist regime in Poland, had entered into collaboration with President Reagan, who provided him with confidential information about Poland. John Paul II was sensitive to the criticisms and concerns of the United States, who saw its influence diminishing on the Catholic continent.

In May 1980, prior to the election of Ronald Reagan, the Santa Fe Document, prepared by influential right-wing ideologues, argued that:

> [...] United States foreign policy must combat and not only react *a posteriori* against Liberation Theology as it is used in Latin America by the liberation theologian Clergy. The role of the Church in Latin

9. Nelson Rockefeller, United States Department of State, *Bulletin*, December 9, 1969.

> America is vital to the concept of political freedom. Unfortunately, Marxist-Leninist forces have utilized the church as a political weapon against private property and productive capitalism by infiltrating the religious community with ideas that are less Christian than Communist.[10]

In 1984, Cardinal Ratzinger published his first warning against liberation theology, caricaturing and condemning the current of thought. Theologians Leonardo Boff and Gustavo Gutiérrez were put under investigation. The harassment would continue in thousands of ways.

We who lived in Latin America had realized, since the accession of John Paul II, that the rise of the Church of the poor would meet powerful resistance. After riding the crest of the momentum of the Council, we would now have to navigate in the trough of the wave. Rome's offensive took as a pretext the use of the Marxist analysis of reality, but the real reason, in my opinion, was the spectacular advance of the laity—especially the poor—who had reappropriated the Church as the People of God on the march. The poor were no longer content to be the mere objects of the charity of the Church, they became active subjects. The ecclesiastical monopoly on power was threatened. Then, a reactionary about-face was engineered in the orientation of the Catholic Church, the control of which was brought firmly back into the sacristy, that is, into the inner sanctum. John Paul II, the superstar pope, adeptly took his evangelism campaign on the road, staging large religious shows around the world, eclipsing the local bishops. The Church of the poor entered on the road to the catacombs.

10. The Committee of Santa Fe, *A New Inter-American Policy for the Eighties* (Washington, D.C.: Council for Inter-American Security (CIS), 1980).

Firmly loyal to the Second Vatican Council

I am the son of the Council, faithful to its teaching, and I can't accept that we should reject that grace. In quiet rebellion, unpretentious and freely, throughout my pan-American travels, I was propelled into action by the inspiration of the Council.

Having provided some idea of the social and political context of Latin America and the dynamics set in motion by Vatican II, I can now continue the story of my mission in Ecuador.

6

A Year in Transition

Questions in need of answers

In Haiti, it was easy to connect with people. I had learned how to express myself in the Creole language that I loved. I had fraternal relationships with our students and we had created a great community, simple though it was. At the parish, I worked alongside Sando, whom I admired for his openness and simplicity, and with Eddy and William, two Haitian priests who had become great friends. The new Haitian priests who had just returned from Canada were involved in work in the parishes: Danis in Léogane, Smith in Saint-Joseph, Yves in Cap-Haïtien, Eddy in Irois. I travelled the roads and trails of the north, west and south by bus and by mule, accompanying for weeks at a time three of the new bishops in their first pastoral visits. On occasion, I visited the Oblates working in the hinterland. I was really happy, and it never occurred to me that I would one day have to leave such fine people.

However, my questions remained unanswered. Why was there so much misery, the dictatorship, Duvalier's repression against his people? Why wasn't there a revolt? How had Haitians maintained their sense of humour? A feeling of powerlessness paralysed me. Why was I here? What should I do? I was conscious that I had not been prepared for my mission and I considered myself lucky not to have lost my faith ... or my mind. When I left Haiti, I was determined to start over again, no matter where. The consumer society into which we were plunging headlong in Quebec seemed irreconcilable with the extreme human suffering that I had just witnessed. It was tempting to totally reject the developed world from which I came.

An invitation to Ecuador

During the summer of 1969, I had a chance encounter with the Ecuadorian Bishop of Latacunga, Mario Ruiz Navas, who was visiting Canada. He needed priests.

"How many foreigners do you have in your clergy?" I asked him.

"None. All our priests are Ecuadorians, and we need people. I think you'd be just the person to take charge of the youth ministry."

"I'm your man. I'll join you in the fall."

The invitation was to come to Ecuador and live and work in indigenous communities. I was attracted to the idea that I wasn't destined for another enclave of Quebec missionaries. I would have to see the country through the eyes of people different than myself if I wanted to learn to live among them.

A month in the land of the Innu[1]

During this transition year, while I reconstituted my intestinal flora that had been destroyed by a case of typhoid, I was asked to serve as a spiritual advisor to the Oblate Missionaries of Mary Immaculate in Quebec and the United States in their efforts to integrate the achievements of the Council into the reality of

1. The Innu are Aboriginal people living on the Lower North Shore of the St. Lawrence River and in the Lac-Saint-Jean region in Quebec.

the secular institutes, as laypeople had finally been accorded, it was believed, status as full members of the Church. Before I left for Ecuador in November, I was sent to visit the Oblates of Schefferville and the Lower North Shore, between Sept-Îles and Blanc-Sablon. There, I discovered the existence of the Innu Nation on their territory of Nitassinan.[2]

I set out from Sept-Îles on the *Fort Mingan*, a five-hundred-fifty kilometre journey that would bring me to the mouth of the great Saint-Augustin River at Pakuashipi. I brought along the books on Marxism I had purchased at the Russian pavilion at Expo 67, counting on having plenty of long quiet days before my departure for Ecuador in November.

On board, I met Rémi Savard, a young anthropologist who planned to accompany a group of Innu hunters during the winter. He was travelling with Alexis Joveneau, a Belgian Oblate who had spent forty years in service to the community of La Romaine as priest. Over the quiet autumn weeks, I had the opportunity to discover a good-natured, silent and closely-knit people. My first encounter with them was in Pakuashipi, where I met a group of sixteen nomadic families who were preparing to spend their last winter in tents: the following year, the federal government planned to build houses for them and get them to settle down. They were very distressed to have to change their lifestyle. Alexis Joveneau invited me to visit the families' tents and meet them.

"But I won't be able to understand them!"

"Don't worry, they'll appreciate your visit. They are a silent people; they don't speak just to hear the sound of their own voices."

Armed with the only word I knew, I entered the first tent.

"*Kuei Kuei*!"

The woman replied with a smile and motioned for me to sit down. She continued her work, and the kids looked at me, laugh-

2. Nitassinan is an immense territory in eastern Quebec that is the ancestral homeland of the Innu.

ing. After a few minutes, embarrassed enough, I waved good-bye and left. I had evidently just gotten off the ship from another planet, suddenly realizing—at the age of thirty—that these people had inhabited this land for eight thousand years. How is it possible for two peoples to live side by side without ever meeting? Why are Aboriginal peoples invisible to us?

That evening, we were invited to hear the old storyteller, Pien Peters. We sat in the dark, on a carpet of fir boughs, leaning against each other. Silence reigned as the grandfather lit his pipe and slowly drew in a few breaths. After a long time, he began to speak in Innu. A woman from the community served as my translator. Over the course of the evening, the storyteller detailed the travels of his band, which every year left the Gulf of St. Lawrence in the fall and headed into the territories to hunt caribou all winter. They travelled on snowshoes all over the great North of Quebec, sometimes all the way to James Bay where they married off their daughters. This immense territory of Nitassinan, the Aboriginals knew like the back of their hands and could name in their own language all the places, rivers and lakes that occupied it.

On the return trip, I travelled by boat, stopping along the shore, at the slow pace of the old coastal traders. The landscape was wild and beautiful. Fjords, tundra, the sea, infinite space, breathtaking freedom! There were two communities in Natashquan: one of Acadian fishermen and one Aboriginal. The Oblates ran a school for the Innu. The night of my arrival, some families came to greet the visitor. In the community room of the missionaries' residence, people sat on the floor along the walls. They greeted us warmly, smiling, without ever looking at us. Indeed, looking someone in the eye is for them a gesture of defiance or arrogance. One's eyes should be kept lowered. At one part of the evening, sitting on a rocking chair, I was welcomed without anyone speaking to me. I confess that for a verbal person such as myself, the situation was embarrassing. The next day I was alone; the Oblates were in school. A well-built young man in his early twenties approached me:

"I've come to see you," he told me in French.

I immediately invited him to take a seat, remembering what Joveneau had told me: "Don't try to converse; they will watch you, but don't force the conversation."

For two hours we gently rocked in our chairs, looking out at the vastness of the sea. Suddenly, he rose to his feet.

"My wife is expecting me for lunch."

I thanked him for his visit, disconcerted. Around two o'clock in the afternoon, he returned, and we resumed where we had left off, the silence punctuated by the creaking of our rocking chairs. In the evening, my friend came back once again:

"My wife sends you this bannock[3] she cooked."

He then left, abruptly. Umpf! The next day, back again. This time, he began the conversation. As a good hunter, he had observed me and taken my measure, like the fox with the Little Prince. He began to speak about his experience. He had gone to college in Sept-Îles and suffered intimidation and racist rejection: "God-damn savage!" He took up boxing to be able to take his place among the others, blessed as he was with fairly impressive physical stature. In front of me, this devastated giant of a man spoke, for two hours, of his humiliation, his suffering, his rejection by white society. He wept bitterly and at length. I was completely shaken; so that's what this young Innu wanted to share with me! The next day I left Natashquan on the *Fort Mingan*, and my young boxer was on board with his wife and child. They were going to Sept-Îles. Throughout the journey, he stood beside me in silence, but now I felt comforted by his wordless presence.

3. Unleavened bread cooked over coals in the sand.

Next stop: Latacunga, Ecuador, via Cuba

It was time to begin my journey to Ecuador. My discovery of the Innu would serve as an introduction to the world of the indigenous people of Ecuador. In Quebec, the War Measures Act was in full force! October 1970 was the scene of an unprecedented political crisis, which culminated in the occupation Quebec by the Canadian Army. Away in northern Quebec, I had somehow missed the news that the army had arrested hundreds of people and that our freedoms had been curtailed. I had brought my Marxist books with me and had taken the time to read and annotate them during my long periods of inactivity. Now what should I do? If the books were discovered in my luggage, I could be arrested as a terrorist. After having lived through the dictatorship in Haiti, I was struck that here in my own country, which I thought immune to such abuse, the situation had suddenly taken a heretofore unimaginable turn. I shipped off my books by mail and returned to Trois-Rivières without any further problems.

My trip to Latin America got underway with a small detour. I had committed myself to preach the Spiritual Exercises to the Oblates in Spanish. My first stop was Cuba where, under the leadership of Matthew Rose, the Cuban missionaries were trying to take their place in the new revolutionary society. Because of the economic blockade, the only gateway to Cuba was then Mexico, which maintained an air link with the island.

I was granted a tourist visa, and booked a hotel in Havana. During the day, I would go and talk with members of the Institute. This had to be done discreetly, because I was not authorized to undertake any religious activity. It was a very stimulating encounter; we debated and discussed the *New Man* that the revolution aspired to bring about. The situation was difficult because basic necessities were rationed. The Cuban Oblates gladly accepted these hardships and wanted to help get their country back on its feet.

When I got to Mexico, I had to ditch my passport, because at the time Ecuador refused to receive travellers from Cuba. I applied for a new passport at the Canadian Embassy and landed in Quito on December 9. I had not forewarned Bishop Ruiz of the date of my arrival; so I took a bus to Latacunga, an hour and a half away, in the Andes. What amazing landscapes! Volcanoes overlooking the Cordillera, cultivated fields lining the mountainsides, unexpected delight at every twist in the winding road. I arrived at my new destination and was received with great affection.

7
The World of the Quichua

Latacunga, Ecuador

In November 1970, having just arrived in Latacunga, a small Andean town at the foot of the Cotopaxi volcano, I was assigned the youth ministry and tasked to set up a chapter of the Young Catholic Students (YCS) among the mestizo college students who were preparing to teach the children of Quichua peasants. The schools for indigenous people were impoverished; teachers would teach a few classes a week in rudimentary windowless straw huts on the Andean highlands known as the Altiplano. The Department of Education was barely a factor in the lives of the masses of illiterate peasants. The marginalization of the indigenous people is the same everywhere, both in the Andes and in Canada. They are the poorest of the poor; marginalized, deprived of all rights, as I was soon to experience firsthand.

An international meeting of the YCS in Lima

Shortly after my arrival, I was informed that an international meeting of the YCS was going to be held in Lima and that I would be a delegate, along with a high school student named Stalin. An auspicious beginning! I had never participated in the Catholic

Action movement[1] as a student and was totally ignorant of the situation in Ecuador. The meeting lasted for ten days, under the leadership of a brilliant university student, Washington Uranga, now a journalist in Argentina. Day after day, listening to the delegations from each country analyse their national sociopolitical reality with the see-judge-act methodology, I began to understand the mechanisms that create poverty, keep people in a state of dependence and prevent genuine development. I discovered the importance of understanding the world in which we live and the need for pastoral work to properly analyse social reality. Poverty was not a natural phenomenon, but social. I went back to Latacunga better prepared, thanks to Washington and Stalin. Young Latin Americans had introduced me to social analysis and contributed to my development as a militant activist.

During our discussions, one subject came up again and again. The youth of Catholic Action became conscious and politicized by reflecting together on reality: see-judge-act is a method that leads to understanding the causes of injustice. It was often the case that when people reached this level of understanding and decided to get involved, they were rejected by their Christian communities. They were cast as revolutionaries, protesters. The observation was made that the Churches were unable to support young people who wanted to change the world and become politically involved. During this revolutionary period, there were many who left the Church after being trained in the Catholic Action movement. Our traditional theology encouraged providing charitable assistance to the poor rather than working to eradicate poverty. One of the challenges I took away from this meeting was to support Christian activists so that their faith in Jesus moved them into committed action in the service of the oppressed.

---

1. A movement of the Catholic Church whose objective is to promote social doctrine through action taken by the laity in different walks of life.

A brutal first contact

My first encounter with the highland communities would not be trivial. The Quichua live on food crops (potatoes, corn, fava beans, onions) and small livestock (llamas, sheep and guinea pigs). The best land in the valley, located about two thousand five hundred metres above sea level between two mountain ranges that cross Ecuador from north to south, traditionally belong to the large mestizo landowners; while the Quichua have been forced to relocate higher and higher—to over three thousand metres in altitude—where the land is covered in snow all year round.

One Sunday, the bishop asked me to invite the highland communities to attend a course on sheep farming. Through Caritas, we had imported some Australian breeding sheep and organized, under the auspices of the diocesan Church, a one-week course for people from the indigenous communities who wanted to improve the quality of their depleted livestock. Since I do not speak Quichua, Sara, a nun, accompanied me as an interpreter. Off I went to recruit interns in the highlands for a course on "sheep-ology." When I saw their faces, I immediately realized that people were either suspicious or upset. I asked to meet with the authorities of the hamlet and deliberated through my translator. During my third visit to the third community, things started to heat up. A hundred furious people surrounded my jeep as soon as I arrived. I tried to speak, but the faces were tense and hostile. People had been drinking and were aggressive. It was impossible to retreat. A man called out to me in Spanish: "Who do you think you are? Do you think you have the solution to our problems? Perhaps we don't have letters [referring to their illiteracy], but we have memories. Priests—that's something we know about around here."

I had absolutely no idea what he meant, but I was frozen with fear. People were becoming increasingly belligerent and closed in on me, threatening. Sara, white as an altar cloth, spoke to them gently in Quichua; I really believe she was my guardian angel that day. Suddenly, she gestured for me to jump in the jeep and we backtracked to the highway in panic. A bottle smashed into the windshield, but we were safe. I had made my missionary entry into the Andes.

The next day, the community's chief came to apologize to the bishop. He had not been there the day before. The landowner had told the peasants that a communist priest would try to lure them to the city so he could steal their land in their absence. The landlord gave them alcohol to get them drunk. They were waiting for me. I also learned that the region's religious communities had, for centuries, "owned" land and "Indians," that they had dealt harshly with their "serfs" and even whipped them until recently. Obviously, the indigenous people had not forgotten. I would soon realize that their situation was intolerable.

Centuries of oppression

In the greatest destitution, on land exposed to the cold, wind and rain of the highlands, in dark huts of wet straw, without access to schools worthy of the name, often without roads or drinking water, the Quichua lived for five hundred years as slaves to unscrupulous landlords, alienated by a Catholic religion that demanded their tithes and offerings to maintain the Church and keep them under submission. All too often, the clergy acted as oppressors of the Quichua people. The peasants had to pay a tithe before confession and communion at Easter; to the priest went the first fruits of the harvest; they were subjected to community service—without compensation—for the construction of chapels and other Church buildings; every religious service, from baptisms to funerals, had its price.

Article 68 of the first Constitution of the Republic (1830), designated the priests as "tutors and natural parents of the innocent, abject and miserable indigenous people."[2] The Catholic religion then being the state religion, the Church served as a pillar of the Spanish domination of the indigenous peoples, a reality that was never questioned until the Latin American Bishops' Conference in Medellin in 1968.

Sent to Pujilí

After hearing the story of this first traumatic experience over a gin toddy, the bishop suggested that I go and live in Pujilí, a gloomy village of dried mud brick walls and narrow cobblestone streets; home to a large, dark colonial church with very thick walls. My amiable Ecuadorian companion, Holguer, and I were introduced by the bishop the following Sunday at High Mass in a church filled to the brim with indigenous people wearing red ponchos. The village's personalities sat in the front: the mayor, the notables and church ladies all dressed in black and veiled in lace mantillas. Holguer and I celebrated the Mass without ecclesiastical garments.

"I am here today to introduce you to the two priests who will be in your service," said the bishop. "They are not dressed in cassocks as an indication of how things are changing. Above all, I am sending these priests to serve the thirty-five Quichua communities of the parish, who have been sorely neglected in the past. You will have to get used to not seeing much of them in the village; they will be spending most of their time in the countryside."

The bishop's message was clear: the indigenous communities would be his priority.

On Sunday market day I'd wait in the rectory office to receive the parishioners, who came down from the hills with their llamas loaded with products to sell. Barefoot women, weighed down

2. Constitution of the Republic of Ecuador. Comparative Constitutions Project.

by kilos of produce, carrying their infants on their backs and dragging two or three children glued to their skirts, smiled sadly. These peasants had come to offer a Mass stipend or schedule the celebration of a baptism or a wedding. To be certain that the priest would be able to understand them, they had hired a bilingual mestizo from the village and, together with this fake lawyer, timidly entered the office, knelt and kissed the blessing hand of the *Padrecito*, the diminutive of "Father" used to address priests. When they gave us their hands, the men were careful to wrap them in their ponchos so as not to contaminate us with their rough peasant's hands. I was shocked! Such debasement seemed totally inappropriate. They did not have to pay to talk to me. In the future, I would firmly show these opportunistic "intermediaries" the door.

"Sir," I said to the peasant, "you are an honest man, you work hard and you are entitled to respect. I am your brother; let's shake hands like men. You speak pretty good Spanish while I am ignorant, I do not know how to speak Quichua. But I promise you I'll learn."

My colleague and I decided to put an end to these demeaning colonial and patriarchal customs: I was put off by how the priests spoke to the peasants, using the familiar pronouns and calling them *mi hijito, mi hijita*, "My little child." This condescending attitude revealed a deep-seated racism.

On the ground floor in the rectory, there were large unoccupied rooms that were made available the night before market day to families who, arriving at night, would otherwise have had to sleep outdoors, exposed to the weather. From Coronita, a Colombian nun who had lived among the indigenous people for thirty years, I started learning the language of the Incas. I had trouble accepting that, for the priests of the diocese, learning Quichua was not a priority. Only one of them knew how to speak it. For five hundred years, the so-called good news had been proclaimed in Spanish, a language that was foreign to them.

Folk religion

Our parish extended to the summit of the Andes and every morning I went to Isinchi to celebrate a Mass for the baby Jesus. Every day of the year, the relatives and neighbours of a different indigenous family would gather for a pilgrimage to this colonial chapel, hung with beautiful paintings from the eighteenth century. The baby Jesus was considered miraculous since it was claimed he was growing. In fact, the owner had sold the chapel's colonial-era statue of Jesus to a collector for a large sum of money and replaced it with a kitsch plaster Jesus that was a bit larger. Hence the miracle of the growing child. With my iconoclastic mentality, it's not surprising that I did not put much faith in these devotions. However, a peasant had warned me: "Don't ever mess with the customs of the people."

Whereas in Quebec we had abandoned the devotions and novenas, in Ecuador, I was immersed in folk religion, incense and holy water. My companion Holguer and I were determined to respect the people's beliefs and to take advantage of the opening that this provided us to shed light on the underlying problems they faced. So every morning, I would set out over the unpaved roads in my Volkswagen Beetle to celebrate the "baby Jesus." I would invariably run across a Saint Joseph, a Virgin Mary, the Magi mounted on llamas, accompanied by real shepherds herding their sheep. After Mass, we would file out in procession, wading through the mud and dung in my white alb, singing Christmas carols. Angels in the fields, no less! A brass band accompanied the little Jesus with noisy pomp, and the pop-pop-pop cadence of fireworks echoed through the mountains.

These religious festivals that the people were so attached to set them back an arm and a leg. The chapel belonged to a female landowner who demanded the lion's share: you had to pay for the red carpet, the band, the choir made up of her three daughters, not to mention the attending priest. The poor struggled to pay for a party that sometimes lasted a week with guests, food and rotgut. This often gave rise to collective drunkenness, violence, and was a dramatic factor leading to bankruptcy. Truly exploitive!

One morning, I decided to remove the baby Jesus from his golden shrine. I placed him on my arm and went up to a young mother who was holding a beautiful baby with red cheeks and bright black eyes.

"*Guagua cuhai* (let me hold the baby)."

"He'll cry," she replied nervously.

I placed the baby on my other arm.

"My friends, you have come here to worship the baby Jesus."

They all watched me, silent and impenetrable. I held two children in my arms: "Which of them seems more important to you?"

"The Child-God, *taita amito* (little master)."

"Go ahead and touch it, ma'am. What is the statue of baby Jesus made of?"

She touched it, shyly.

"It's made of plaster."

"And now, please go ahead and touch this baby. Is he made out of wood? (Laughter.) You have a beautiful devotion, you have come to pay homage to the baby Jesus; but it is only an image. This child of yours is worth much more than this beautiful image. Look at this baby, he's truly beautiful! You are believers, people who serve the Creator with great faith. Your children are the children of God, in flesh and bones. You are spending a lot of money for this festival, and the landowners and the priest will take the profits. This has to stop. God has no need for your money; He wants you to live like human beings, not like animals. From now on, you will not have to pay the priest for your devotions; it will be free, and you can leave a gift that you can afford in the church poor box. In the future, we are going to ask the owner to give the chapel back to the parish. We do not want a religion that abuses the poor. Look at your women, they go barefoot while the men wear shoes. Your children are undernourished. God's will requires that you put your resources at the service of your loved ones."

The organizer of the festival rose with dignity; he asked to speak and then thanked me for opening his eyes. He wept profusely, apologizing. There were repercussions to what had happened: the owner of the chapel screamed with indignation; she forbid us from returning to the chapel and instead—at her own expense—hired a holy religious priest from town to serve in our stead. The bishop then imposed a ban on the shrine, and the good lady lost this lucrative source of income. We had touched on a wound that had been eating away at the Church for centuries: the alliance of the powerful and rich with the clergy. But a number of priests accused us of wanting to ruin "the best" parish of the diocese.

The army topples President Velasco

February 14, 1972, a night of terrible flooding when even the rats were curled up in their holes, I was awakened by martial music playing at full volume. Boom, boom! Boom, boom! I tried to see out my window overlooking Pujilí's central square, but all was dark and the rain fell in buckets.

Suddenly, piercing the din of the storm, a hoarse voice bellowed through the speakers of the town hall across the square: "Attention! Attention! People of Pujilí, President Velasco Ibarra has abandoned his post and cowardly fled the country."

Martial music. Half an hour later: "Attention! Attention! Following the abandonment of the country by Velasco, General Guillermo Rodriguez Lara, in the patriotic spirit that characterizes him, has agreed to assume the reins of power."

The military succeeded at their coup, and the new dictator was actually our next-door neighbour. In fact, the general had been born in Pujilí and owned a large estate on the outskirts of the parish. His residence in the village was right next to ours.

The coup took place in relative calm, without killing or violent excesses, because the repression was aimed at Velasco's political party. The general was defined as a supporter of the moderate left who wanted Ecuador's oil used for the development of the country's infrastructure.

The village of Pujilí prepared a large welcome. The mayor, the general's brother-in-law, spared no expense. A parade of students in uniform was organized. However, the general's holdings included a large amount of land where some two thousand five hundred Quichua lived as his serfs. His land and farm were located eighteen kilometres from the village, accessed by a dirt road in very poor condition. Juihua was a *huasipungo*[3] where there was no drinking water and no school. The council of elders came to see me before the event: the Quichua wanted to march in front of their *patron* and take the opportunity to seek improvements in their living conditions. I gladly agreed to march, dressed like them, in a red poncho and a hat.

But the mayor wouldn't hear of it: there was no way there was going to be any marching ponchos. Out of the question! I called Bishop Ruiz, who was a friend of the general. The bishop agreed to speak with the general, and ask him to let the indigenous people march. The general accepted, provided that there would be no demands. With the youth of the YCS, we made a banner that read: "The 2,500 peasants of Juihua, with no road, no water and no school, greet the President of the Republic." When we arrived near the square, the security forces tore up the banner. In front of the dignitaries' platform, I waved to the general. There was a burst of laughter among the spectators to see the gringo wearing a red poncho. Taking advantage of this distraction, I opened a breach in the line of soldiers and mounted the platform to greet

3. The *huasipungo* is a feudal system maintained by the large landowners. The farmers work without pay and receive in exchange for their labour the use of a marginal piece of land, from which they try to eke out a living.

the president, taking with me the Quichua leader. In front of this friendly audience, I asked the general to listen to the wishes of his "Indians." The indigenous leader took the microphone and, with deft diplomacy and clever humour, challenged Ecuador's new strongman to begin by making reforms in his own backyard. President Rodriguez had to promise, in front of everyone present, to set a good example.

The "Bishop of the Indians"

The Young Christian Students chapter organized mestizos who were conscious of the racism in which they had been raised, and with enthusiasm and creativity they struggled to raise the awareness of the people of the village that racism could be fought. I met one of them in Paris forty years later through the Internet, who told me about that time: "You helped me to discover the reality of the indigenous people—whom I had played with since I was born—when I was seventeen. We didn't realize what was going on around us. Later, I became an anthropologist and I have dedicated my life to studying the Quichua communities."

A workshop with the students was held near Riobamba, in an indigenous education centre. There, I would meet someone I had heard about since my arrival, Bishop Leonidas Proaño, a man who had devoted his ministry to improving the lives of the indigenous people and to fighting against the racism that these communities had been subjected to from the time of the colony. He was a man of great simplicity and his evangelical discourse inspired anyone thirsting for justice. We listened eagerly to what he said; his wisdom and courage inspired us.

His fellow bishops, on the other hand, were generally quite hostile and looked down on him from on high, with the happy exception of the Cardinal of Quito and our own bishop, Mario Ruiz, who supported him. The Vatican Ambassador to Ecuador, Papal Nuncio Accogli, led a campaign to vilify Proaño in Rome, including a number of charges that were subsequently proved false and unfounded. Accogli tried to get him expelled from Riobamba, thus serving the interests of the landowners. The youth organized demonstrations and wrote letters of support, which were sent to the Church authorities, demanding hands off the "Bishop of the Indians." Proaño continued his work with determination and humility. In him I discovered a prophet, whose path I was to cross once again decades later and whose influence would be crucial on my personal journey.

Indigenous rights violated

When you arrive in a new country, you can be shocked by certain behaviours that the local people are accustomed to and do not even notice. Thus, as I gradually explored the province of Cotopaxi, I could not understand why the Ecuadorian priests seemed to feel no need to speak Quichua with the indigenous people, who formed a large part of the population.

The peasants themselves were ashamed to speak their own language and tried to speak in halting Spanish. Racism was rampant. One evening, as I returned to Quito on a crowded intercity bus, a group of mestizos on the side of the road motioned for the driver to stop so they could get on. The bus was full, and so, without a moment's hesitation, he pointed to a Quichua family and asked them to get off. The Quichua did as he asked, and the mestizos got on. I was furious and got off the bus. Embarrassed, the driver asked me to get back on, but I insisted that the Quichua family get on with me. It was the practice that indigenous people were frequently asked to relinquish their seats to mestizos. Women, who had the care of young children, stood up and stayed standing for the rest of the journey that they had duly paid for.

One morning I came across three men with a teenager lying on a makeshift stretcher. He was suffering from acute peritonitis, and they asked me to give him the last rites. The boy was sixteen; he was feverish, his belly swollen and purplish, and he was writhing in pain.

"He is an orphan," they said. "Our family has been raising him. We are returning from the hospital in Latacunga; they gave us aspirin for his pain and told us to bring him home to die."

My blood ran cold.

"That's not what's going to happen. We need to get in the road and flag down a vehicle. We're going back to the hospital."

A truck agreed to take us there; the poor boy whimpered over the fifteen miles of bad road, lying in the back of the truck.

At the emergency room entrance, an employee hastened to warn us that we could not enter. The surgeon was preparing to leave.

"You sent this young man away because he is poor and indigenous; you're going to operate on him immediately. Otherwise, you'll face prosecution for refusing care to a person in distress. You've taken an oath, doctor!"

The doctor agreed, embarrassed. The next day when I arrived at the hospital to visit, the boy, smiling, had yanked out the tubes in his nose and said he was ready to go. He was ok! Later on, with the leaders of the community, we analysed what had happened.

"Stop bending over and putting up with such contempt. As farmers, you produce food for all the people of Ecuador. You are citizens, demand your rights be respected, unite!"

That was the last thing that happened to me before leaving Pujilí.

A mission cut short

My time in Ecuador was all too short; at the end of my second year there, on Christmas Eve, I was hospitalized in Guayaquil, a tropical city with a very hot climate. Typhoid fever kept me bedridden until just before Easter; a bout of illness that left me in a weakened state. I went back to Quebec for a prolonged rest, without having had the time to do what I had hoped.

Life is a wonderful teacher: in only a couple of months, I had been introduced to social analysis and the world of the first peoples and their desire to live on their land with dignity and freedom. In Haiti, I had learned to rail against injustice, without knowing why it exists. Now I began to understand what kind of world I lived in. And it was the Ecuadorian students that had helped me to make this leap forward. No university could have taught me as quickly. Now that I had experienced it first-hand and had reached certain conclusions, it was time to move to the third phase: action. I now felt much better prepared to fulfill my work as a missionary.

8

Proaño, the "Bishop of the Indians"

Before turning the page on Ecuador, I want to return to the figure of Leonidas Proaño, prophet and pastor of the Amerindians.[1] At the time we met in 1971, he was being aggressively harassed by the Riobamba elites—mainly the large landowners—who saw the advancement of indigenous rights as a threat to their interests. Serious charges against Proaño were regularly brought before the Roman Curia who eventually sent, some years later, an apostolic visitor to investigate their minister. He was totally exonerated and even commended for his work.

But what, in fact, was he charged with? When Proaño arrived in the province of Chimborazo[2] in 1962, the Diocese of Riobamba had two hundred seventy-six thousand inhabitants, seventy percent of whom were Quichua. They typically owned from two to five acres of land per family, while the farms of large landowners exceeded two thousand five hundred acres. In 1971, the bishop explained his pastoral aim: the liberation of the people of Chimborazo and the construction of a community Church in service of this liberation.

He told us why he had refused to rebuild the cathedral destroyed by an earthquake: "I'm on the side of the poorest of

1. I have mainly drawn my information from the biography written by Giovanni Ferrò, *Taita Proaño*, Quito, 2010

2. Chimborazo, the highest volcano in the Ecuadorian Andes, peaks at 6,268 metres in altitude.

the poor in their just struggle for their rights to the land. The cathedral I want to build will not be made of stone, it will be a living cathedral, a living Church due to the birth of the indigenous movement that is struggling to build a new society."

All the resources and efforts of the Church of Riobamba were invested in the education of the illiterate rural population. Riobamba community radio, broadcast in all the area's hamlets and villages, enabled the Quichua to learn to read and write, become educated, get organized, and to communicate among themselves to revitalize their language, Quichua, which is spoken in the Andes by more than ten million indigenous people from Columbia to northern Argentina.

The development of training centres, community radio that covered the entire territory of the province and moral and financial support of the diocesan Church, a respected institution, all favoured the formation and development of an organized indigenous movement that slowly took shape. The Riobamban elites felt their secular domination threatened and vehemently attacked the person they referred to as the communist bishop, since everything in their world had reached the tipping point.

Proaño defended himself, pointing out that Catholic Action had taught him to analyse reality.

"See, judge, act," he said. "I've come to really believe in this method. See reality. Look at it in all its dimensions. Seek its root causes. Then make a judgment on it, that is to say a comparison between what is and what should be, between this reality and God's plan. Finally, act. This means making resolutions to change the reality in accord with the Divine Plans. In recent years when I was being slandered as a communist and a Marxist, I thought back to what I had learned from the Young Christian Students' method. I also thought that my critics were wrong in their accusations, unaware as they were that I had become accustomed over many years to knowing and analysing reality in order to arrive, through reflection, at a real commitment for change."

Taita Proaño, as he was affectionately called by the Quichua, dreamed of a fully indigenous church.

"Evangelism [...] failed in five hundred years to penetrate the soul of Amerindian culture. [...] This evangelizing deficiency is the root cause of the fact that no indigenous Church has appeared to date and that the Church has been accused up to the present of promoting the unjust domination of the imposed culture."

The Latin American Bishops' Conference in Medellin strongly supported the difficult path that Proaño had embarked on. Indeed, the bishops advocated nothing less than to "defend the rights of the poor and oppressed according to the Gospel commandment"[3] and "energetically denounce the abuses and unjust consequences of the excessive inequalities between poor and rich, weak and powerful." The pastors finished with a personal commitment: "We wish our houses and style of life to be modest, our clothing simple, our works and institutions functional, without show or ostentation."[4] These resolutions were reflected in the life of the "Bishop of the Indians"; he didn't just pay lip service to them.

Proaño attends the synod

In 1971, Pope Paul VI convened a synod in Rome to discuss the life of priests and justice in the world. The crisis of the clergy was very deep: after the Council, in fact, tens of thousands of priests left the ministry, often to marry. Since 1967, according to data from the Holy See, more than seventy thousand priests left the ministry. This figure is conservative; the number could be closer to eighty or one hundred thousand, according to organizations of married priests.

In Quito, the Episcopal Conference met to appoint two delegates to the synod. The Ecuadorian priests wanted Proaño

3. *Medellin Document*, Peace, Nos. 22 and 23.
4. *Medellin Document*, Poverty of the Church, No. 3.

to represent them because of his social commitment and his position on celibacy of priests. Proaño's view was that mandatory celibacy was an obstacle to an indigenous church and, year after year, he asked Rome's permission to ordain married men. Hundreds of priests met in the building of the Episcopal Conference in Quito and in general session, elected representatives to send to the Conference, arguing that if the synod was to be about the life of priests, it was appropriate that they choose the bishops they wanted to represent them. They demanded that Proaño be among the group. The prelates dug in their heels and refused any further dialogue with their clergy. Finally, to resolve the conflict, Pope Paul VI intervened and appointed the Bishop of Riobamba on his own.[5] Proaño had a great influence on the synod delegates' Roman document, "Justice in the World," published without being censored by the Roman Curia. The text solemnly affirmed that:

> Action on behalf of justice and participation in the transformation of the world fully appear to us as a constitutive dimension of the preaching of the Gospel, or, in other words, of the Church's mission for the redemption of the human race and its liberation from every oppressive situation.[6]

Riobamba, twenty years later

I left Ecuador in April 1972, but Ecuador, and especially the Quichua communities, never left me. It took twenty years before I finally returned with twenty-two students from Quebec. I was working as a spiritual advisor to the Mouvement des étudiants

---

5. It is interesting to note that at this same synod the Canadian bishops, through the voice of Cardinal George B. Flahiff, Archbishop of Edmonton, proposed the establishment of an international commission to study the issue of the access of women to the priesthood.

6. *Justice in the World*, No. 7 [online]. [http://www.shc.edu/theolibrary/resources/synodjw.htm]

chrétiens du Québec (MECQ) (Quebec Christian Student Movement), on college and university campuses.

Near Montreal, in the summer of 1990, the Oka crisis erupted; for seventy-eight days the Mohawks of Kanesatake and Kahnawake confronted the provincial police and the Canadian Army, in defense of their autonomy. These events, widely publicized and hypocritically manipulated by the provincial and federal governments, led to a great deal of animosity among the Quebec population and a major upsurge of racism directed towards the eleven First Nations living in Quebec. Since MECQ had participated in the demonstrations in support of the claims of the Aboriginals, we decided to take a group of Quebec students to do an internship in first peoples' communities in Ecuador to broaden their understanding of indigenous people. During the 1990-91 school year, we organized two groups, one in Chicoutimi and the other in Quebec City, and in July, travelled to Ecuador for a period of seven weeks. This trip had a profound impact on the students' subsequent life choices.

What a joy to find myself back in the country twenty years later and to be able to see how far the indigenous people had come! I saw how Proaño's dream had spread far beyond the borders of Chimborazo province. The students from Quebec, who participated in the daily work in the fields, were hosted by indigenous families. Two large organizations received us with open arms and shared their experiences with us, how they were organized and what their objectives were: ECUARUNARI (the Confederation of Peoples of Quichua Nationality of Ecuador) and CONAIE (the Confederation of Indigenous Nationalities of Ecuador), which coordinated the organizations of all the indigenous nationalities and black organizations in the country. The Amerindians had become politically organized and fully engaged in the struggle for a plurinational and multicultural state.

Workshops with the Quichua peasants

Bishop Victor Corral, Proaño's chosen successor, whom I had known in Latacunga in 1970, invited me to conduct Bible education workshops for the leaders of the mestizo and indigenous Christian communities in the rural areas. I went to Casa de Santa Cruz twice, in 1992 and 1993. This learning centre for laypeople had been founded by the Diocese of Riobamba to teach indigenous people who were able to reflect on their Christian faith and embody it in the Quichua culture. I first made contact with Delfín Tenesaca, a peasant of great wisdom, who was at the time director of the Centre for Pastoral and Social Education at Santa Cruz. He was one of the "theologians in sandals" taught by Proaño with an eye towards establishing an indigenous Church. I was awestruck by the depth shown by these people who, without giving up their work in the fields, had deepened Catholic theology and had rethought it from the foundation of their own values. Another theologian, Carlos Zambrano, revealed that God had not arrived in Ecuador with the Spaniards, as they had claimed.

"For millennia," said Carlos Zambrano, "we have been in contact with the Creator, Pachacamac. We worship Mother Earth and we offer to the Creator what she procures for us. When the Europeans arrived with their arrogance, they took us for savages and treated us barbarically. They beat us down with their Bible, claiming that our situation of slavery was for our own good. We have never been orphans of God, who has always accompanied our ancestors."

Carlos went on to study law at the University of Quito, an institution where "Indians" were not welcome. He was asked to remove his poncho to avoid trouble, and he flatly refused.

"I am studying law to defend OUR rights. I am Quichua and I am proud to identify myself by my poncho."

The workshops that I had been asked to lead took place during a one-month internship of thirty men and women farmers of all ages. It's objective—at the request of Bishop Corral—was to reconcile the Quichua with the Bible, which had been imposed on them through violence and which they were reluctant to accept. It must be remembered that the invasion of the Europeans in 1492 with its "Christian civilization" brought, in its wake, the genocide of sixty million indigenous people in the Americas, the largest known genocide in human history.

During his visit to Peru in 1988, John Paul II received a somewhat unexpected gift: a Bible!

> We, Indians of the Andes and America, decided to take advantage of John Paul II's visit to return to him his Bible because in five centuries it has given us neither love, nor peace, nor justice. Please, take your Bible and give it back to our oppressors, because they need its moral precepts more than we. Since the arrival of Christopher Columbus, the Bible was imposed upon America with force: European culture, language, religion, and values. The Bible came to us as part of imposed colonial change. It was the ideological arm of the colonial assault. The Spanish sword, which by day attacked and assassinated the body of the Indians, by night changed itself into the cross which attacked the Indian soul.[7]

Hoping to contribute to their search for identity, I decided to re-read the Bible with the Quichua. They are spiritual people and thirsty for knowledge. We reviewed all the texts of the Genesis creation narrative, comparing them to the creation stories found in the Inca culture. We re-read the biblical texts describing the violence that took place against women and it led us to reflect on the relationships between men and women

---

7. Pablo Richard, "Hermenéutica bíblica india: Revelación de Dios en las religiones indígenas y en la Biblia (Después de 500 años de dominación)," in *Sentido histórico del V Centenario* (1492–1992), ed. Guillermo Meléndez (San José: CEHILA- DEI, 1992), 45–62. Cited by Elsa Tamez, "The Bible and the Five Hundred Years of Conquest," in R.S. Sugirtharahaj, ed., *Voice from the Margin*. Orbis Books, New York: 2006.

in Quichua communities; at the end of the course, the female participants thanked me for raising this issue. We also reflected on the role an indigenous church would play by re-reading the Acts of the Apostles in the light of the experiences of the base communities. We succeeded in establishing an open dialogue between the biblical message and indigenous culture.

In the class there were only men and women of the earth. Contrary to their usual everyday routines, they remained seated for long periods; the stillness numbed their bodies, accustomed as they were to hard agricultural labour, but they vigorously fought it off. If I suggested taking a break, they immediately protested. Their thirst for knowledge was impressive. They carefully and slowly noted everything in their notebooks, meticulously forming the letters with effort. Spanish was hard for them, laborious. I'd speak for a few minutes, then a bilingual member of the group would take over in Quichua. By the end of the day, I was shot, since for hours on end I hadn't understood a thing, with my limited comprehension of Quichua. From time to time, I would ask for an explanation, which they provided with patience and respect. The experience showed me how the biblical texts speak to their culture, to their reality. The youngest, José, fifteen, was the most bilingual of them all. Eagerly, he helped others to pass from one language to the other. What a great experience, reading the Bible with people who had such an articulate and authentic spirituality!

Sumak Kawsay, Life in Fullness

Today, in Ecuador, the indigenous people are organized and struggling to rebuild their country on new foundations, by exploring traditional knowledge. The Quichua have succeeded in having *Sumak Kawsay* - Life in Fullness (an Amerindian concept that embraces the full potential of life in a community system) incorporated into the country's constitution. It's more than the idea of improving the existing system to have a better life. Luis Macas, who was Minister of Agriculture, explains that the concept of “Life in Fullness” is actually not adaptable to the current system.

> This is a proposal to go beyond the harmful system in which we live in order to build a community model. [...] We must fundamentally transform the old state structures and institutions in place and build a new society, this time with our own hands, with the hands of the people. This is not a proposal for indigenous people, but for all of humanity. Because we consider that it is an option of building a life for everyone.[8]

These Andean brothers and sisters are calling us to a revolution: to build a world community, where Mother Earth has rights, where all living things are recognized as being interconnected and are therefore protected, where the Living Beings that we are take our place as part of a greater whole. The Quichua cosmological perspective is a fundamental contribution to the future of life on Earth. We would do well to listen carefully.

8. Luis Macas, *El Sumak Kawsay* [online]. [decrecimientoybuenvivir.files.wordpress. com/2011/01/sumak-kawsay-luis-macas.pdf] (December 12, 2013)

Open air Mass; a Quichua peasant makes an offering of grains and water in thanksgiving to Mother Earth.

The working class areas of Santiago started as illegal squats. When the people managed to settle, these neighbourhoods were described as "mushroom settlements," *callampas*, in Spanish.

During the three years of Salvador Allende's Popular Front government, the Chilean people, in political parties, trade unions and community and social organizations, took an active part in the social changes undertaken.

John Paul II visited Chile in 1987 and met with the dictator Augusto Pinochet who claimed to be defending Christian civilization against communism.

On Good Friday, the base communities organized Stations of the Cross processions in the streets of Santiago. Thousands of the faithful prayed in spots that had been hit by repression, thereby linking the Chilean people's suffering with the passion of Christ.

9
Pinochet's Chile

Upon my return from Ecuador, I worked over the next three years as Vicar of the parish of Notre-Dame-de-la-Paix, in Trois-Rivières. Bishop Pelletier, who distrusted missionaries, warned me not to import ideas from South America, but he agreed that I should go to work in this parish, where several priests had refused to be assigned.

Questions about the parish

Since my stay in Haiti, I had been thinking about a number of aspects of the work of parish priests. I wanted to work in an environment where I would be tackling the challenges facing society, fighting for the rights of poor people, working with others to bring about social justice. I was pleased that the parish had no church, because I didn't want to be a guardian of the temple. The parish numbered around five thousand "souls," and we had a relationship only with the hundreds of people who attended Mass. I was suffocating in the parish enclosure; I felt cut off from everyday life. A missionary should not limit himself to performing sacred acts; he should be in service to the world and in the world, by the side of the disempowered. It seemed to me that the life-style demanded of priests isolated us from reality. The way we were expected to live made it difficult for us to understand the lives of people. We didn't get married or raise children, we didn't have a good grasp of what people went through in their work worlds, our emotional life was castrated, we worked on Sundays while everyone else had the day off and our lives were made up of Masses, sacraments, religion and devotions. I longed for a service that was a great deal more embodied in reality and less focused on religion. I decided to break with the parish model; this is what I jokingly call "my divorce." I have great respect and admiration for those who succeed in an exemplary manner to operate within these structures, but it was not what was calling me.

Departure for Chile

Headlining the French-language national news on Radio-Canada on the evening of September 11, 1973, journalist Jean Charpentier reported live from the roof of a hotel overlooking La Moneda, the presidential palace in Santiago, Chile; a military coup was underway. The Chilean Air Force was bombing the government headquarters where the elected president, Salvador Allende, continued to resist until the end. The scene was apocalyptic. This is how democracies are treated when they do not act in the interests of the multinationals! It was a terrible setback for Chile. On Radio Magallanes, just before his death, Allende addressed his people:

> Workers of my country, I have faith in Chile and its destiny. Other men will overcome this dark and bitter moment when treason seeks to prevail. Keep in mind that, much sooner than later, great avenues will again be opened, through which will pass the free man, to construct a better society. Long live Chile! Long live the people! Long live the workers! These are my last words, and I am certain that my sacrifice will not be in vain, I am certain that, at the very least, it will be a moral lesson that will punish felony, cowardice, and treason.[1]

1. In *Monthly Review*, http://mrzine.monthlyreview.org/2006/allende110906.html.

The bombing of La Moneda violently interrupted the socialist experiment the Chilean people had voted for and inaugurated a neoliberal military dictatorship that lasted seventeen long years, under the rule of General Augusto Pinochet. The coup was the means used by the U.S. and Chilean economic elites to restore power to the right. I made up my mind that very night: I would go to Chile to join the resistance. I immediately communicated with the Quebec Foreign Missions Society—which I joined—and on September 29, 1975, I landed in Chile, with clenched teeth and my stomach in knots.

I had already visited Chile on two occasions: the first at the end of 1967 when I was invited by the Oblate lay missionaries to lead spiritual retreats during the regime of Christian Democratic President Eduardo Frei; then again under the government of Salvador Allende in 1971. I had been won over by the people: their grassroots organizations, political vitality and ambitious social projects; including nationalization of the copper mines, agrarian reform, mobilization for the right to social housing and access to health. A wind of freedom was blowing through this country at the end of the world. I had subscribed to the magazine *Mensaje* of the Chilean Jesuits and for fifteen years closely followed what was happening.

But now, everything was changing. After the coup, people hid like rats, persecuted and threatened with death. The sectors of the Church in solidarity with the working masses suffered terrible repression. According to the theologian Pablo Richard, at least one hundred and twenty Catholic priests, thirty evangelical pastors, thirty-five religious brothers and sisters and two hundred secular Christians belonging to the movement for socialism were expelled from Chile, after being detained and tortured in many cases. At least thirty of them were murdered.

The military regime and the Churches clash

A few weeks after my arrival in mid-November 1975, I attended a meeting of the clergy convened by the Cardinal of Santiago, Raúl Silva Enríquez. Several hundred people attended and the atmosphere was tense, as a number of priests had been arrested and repression was being directed against the Catholic and Lutheran churches, very active in the defense of human rights through the Committee for Cooperation for Peace in Chile—COPACHI.

Here was the situation. The secretary general of MIR,[2] Andrés Pascal Allende and his wife, along with activist Nelson Gutiérrez, had successfully evaded an army ambush and had taken refuge in the Embassies of Costa Rica and the Papal Nuncio, respectively. They were exactly the "big fish" that the military wanted to catch at any cost. The priests had hidden Gutiérrez and arranged treatment for his wounds, and had facilitated access to Vatican diplomatic representation. The Papal Nuncio, furious, threatened to hand him over to the authorities. Lengthy negotiations with the local hierarchy and the military regime finally managed to secure safe passage to Sweden.

Two years after the coup, the crackdown was still in full swing, and raids on houses, arbitrary arrests and disappearances continued unabated. Shaken by the intensity of the repression and regretting his support for the military coup, Cardinal Silva resolved to defend the countless victims of repression. With his legal training, he played a key role during this troubled time. Immediately after the coup, he founded, with the bishop of the Lutheran Church, Helmut Frenz, the Human Rights Defense Committee, the forerunner to COPACHI. This organization irritated the military authorities to the greatest degree and on October 3, Helmut Frenz was expelled from Chile.

2. Movimiento de Izquierda Revolucionaria (Revolutionary Left Movement).

During this stormy meeting with the clergy, the cardinal announced that he would comply with the orders of President Pinochet to dissolve COPACHI. Those present at the meeting were furious to see him succumb to the dictatorship on an issue concerning the fundamental right to life and physical integrity. On September 18, Chile's Independence Day, people customarily sing a *Te Deum* in the cathedral, a hymn of thanksgiving to God for the Republic, in the presence of the political authorities. The priests reproached Silva for having held to tradition under such unacceptable circumstances. An old religious priest took the microphone: "Your Eminence, when St. Ambrose saw the Roman Emperor Theodosius enter the cathedral of Milan, he addressed him, saying: 'You cannot enter, because your hands are covered in blood.' This is what we expect of you with the dictator."

After a long silence, Silva replied, unperturbed: "I'm not St. Ambrose and I will never break the bonds that exist between the Church and the Government of Chile."

Following this, the cardinal established the Vicariate of Solidarity, headquartered in a building adjacent to the cathedral. Over the years of the dictatorship, the Vicariate remained for Pinochet a perpetual annoyance and a space where the banned opposition political parties were able to gradually reorganize underground. It was a refuge for the persecuted, who could obtain legal assistance there and a degree of protection. Under the energetic leadership of Cardinal Silva, the Church played a role as a refuge where trade union, community and political organizations managed to adapt and survive.

A new mission in the working-class shantytowns

In the midst of all this conflict and tension, the Quebec Foreign Missions Society priests arrived in Santiago. They had left their Temuco parishes in the south, to come and work in Santiago. The

Medellin document of the Conference of Latin American Bishops wanted a Church that was "authentically poor, missionary and paschal, freed from all temporal power and boldly committed to the liberation of the whole man and of all men."[3] This group of a dozen priests from Quebec had decided to move to the capital to work among the workers and their families in the marginalized communities—the *poblaciones* ("towns" or "villages")—on the outskirts of the city. A few weeks after my arrival, a couple of my companions who had recently moved into the Huamachuco neighbourhood north of the city, René Lapointe and André Drapeau, who were priests from the Saguenay diocese, invited me to stay with them for a while. My initial goals were to get engaged with the world of the impoverished and to get to know the leaders of this progressive Chilean Church.

Large working-class neighbourhoods had arisen along the city's outer perimeter in the 1960s. These shantytowns were called *callampas*, because they spread like mushrooms. Industrialization had forced a large number of peasants to leave the poor and grueling life of the countryside to try to eke out a living in the city. After an initial demographic implosion downtown, thousands of homeless people were organized through the progressive political parties and became squatters in the vineyards and farmlands surrounding Santiago. Precarious encampments, vulnerable to being torn down by the police, were born into unsafe and unclean conditions; little by little, people managed to establish themselves and to secure a minimum of services. Proud of their achievements, the squatters designated their new neighbourhoods with evocative names: La Bandera, La Victoria, Violeta Parra! The city of Santiago became surrounded by an immense crown of *poblaciones*, on the outskirts of a rapidly modernizing megapolis.

---

3. CELAM, *The Church in the Present-Day Transformation of Latin America in the Light of the Council* (Washington, DC: The Latin American Bureau, USCC, 1970).

We Quebecers knew almost nothing about the history of the *poblaciones*, organized at the initiative of the Communist Party, the Socialist Party, the Christian Democrats and the Revolutionary Left Movement (MIR). After the coup, political activists, trade unionists and other social activists were in hiding, on the wanted list and actively being hunted. Detention centres overflowed with political prisoners who were tortured by the security services immediately upon their arrest. Terror stalked the neighbourhoods, and the repression was ruthless. Anyone who had been involved in any way whatsoever in the Allende reforms was threatened.

What difference could three priests from Quebec make in a huge neighbourhood of over thirty thousand people? These new districts had no places of worship. Upon their arrival, my two colleagues had built a wooden chapel, with the determined help of the local residents. As a result, a small network of Christian families began to get active. The nucleus of a small community was born that wanted to be in service to the neighbourhood; the needs were dire and the poverty was wrenching. Our first instinct was to organize base communities. Everyone was talking about them, but no one really knew what they were in practice. Our concerns were pastoral: we dreamed of a Christian community made up of small groups of believers centered around the Bible, assimilating and reflecting on the message of Jesus, and from there, developing solidarity among themselves and with their neighbours. The Conference of Latin American Bishops in Medellin had oriented us on this model of the Church: the base community is "the initial cell of the ecclesiastical structures and the focus of evangelization, and it currently serves as the most important source of human advancement and development."[4]

4. *Ibid*, XV, 10.

A hungry people

In the *callampas*, I met Rachel, a woman in her forties who lived in an outlying camp in a three-by-six-metre shack with her son and daughter, both nearly in their twenties, and her twenty-one year old life companion. This was my first contact with the reality of the underclass. The family lived very poorly in the unheated shack, and Rachel, who suffered from tuberculosis, was very susceptible to bronchitis during the capital's raw winter. Working with her, we started to set up a community kitchen for undernourished children. Rachel, a MIR activist, was an expert organizer. One morning, two mothers with a large wicker basket came to the public market, held twice a week in one of the neighbourhood's streets. They solicited food to prepare the meal of the day. On their cart was written: "This is the hunger of the people!" In the blink of an eye, the police appeared and drove them off, accusing them of insulting the military government and threatening them with jail. There was no hunger in Chile! This experience with Rachel made me aware of the determination of the poor when they organize. The activity of keeping a community kitchen going led directly to demanding the right of working people to a decent job. We were aware that these emergency activities were palliative and risked encouraging people to become dependent. Rachel organized mothers to prepare the meal and got them talking about their rights, and the need for them to unite and organize. It became a place where the spirit of resistance and social consciousness flourished.

At the initiative of the Catholic Church, community kitchens for children spread throughout the country, to the great annoyance of the government, who saw them as a propaganda ploy to embarrass the regime. Gradually, the first lady, Lucia Hiriart de Pinochet, began to organize canteens in competition with the Church. The wife of the dictator played the part of a one-woman Ladies Auxiliary to brand the regime with a charitable image, associating it with the values of the Christian West.

Yes, hunger reigned in the kingdom of Pinochet. In 1976, the regime had removed tariff barriers that protected Chilean products from foreign competition. Chile would be the first to apply to the letter the new market economic standards promoted by the International Monetary Fund. Cheap products from Taiwan immediately flooded the stores and after a few months of this kind of dumping, Chilean manufacturers of textiles, shoes and sundries began to close, one after the other. Meanwhile, state-controlled companies were auctioned off to private companies, which acquired them for a pittance. Working families found themselves unemployed, hungry and with no means to earn an income, while colossal fortunes were amassed from the looting of public assets. Pinochet and his family were the first to profit. Unemployment was endemic.

Training priests to work among the poor

I then contacted Mario Gonzalez, a Chilean priest in his sixties whom Cardinal Silva had tasked to develop theological training that was anchored in the world of the poor, to prepare future priests in the service of the working class. For several years, Mario trained groups of young men who aspired to the priesthood. They lived in small communities in various neighbourhoods and worked for a living while they pursued their theological studies at the university. This seminary project was an urgent response to the need to train pastors who could live among the impoverished and who were prepared to support them in their struggles. I volunteered to take part, and moved into one of the communities.

Mario greeted me with kindness. He was exceptional in his wisdom, openness and good nature. At my request, he introduced me to progressive Chilean priests and sisters from all four corners of the city. With joy, I got to know these inspiring people who chose a radical stance on the side of the disempowered. I was invited to attend "discreet" meetings of people committed to working for justice, kept secret to defend against infiltration by the intelligence services and also because the dictatorship counted on sizeable support among the clergy and the episcopate.

Cardinal Silva returned from a trip to Rome surly and sullen; he summoned the young trainees of the experimental seminar: "It's all over, you're going to be returning to the general theological seminary."

The initiative came to an abrupt halt, as John Paul II put an end to all the experiments in priestly training and returned to the traditional boarding-school approach. Mario learned about the decision when the seminarians came to the meeting, completely shaken. He received the news as a complete betrayal. The cardinal asked him to go into exile to avoid negatively influencing the young people who had looked up to him. With a heavy heart, Mario travelled to Verona, Italy, where he was taken in by a group of worker priests. He returned a year later, struck with terminal cancer that finally took his life on Christmas Day. He and I had planned to work in a new neighbourhood, among the workers and their families, because I had been determined to work with Chileans. I lost a dear friend, I cried a lot. This betrayal of the Church of the poor was to be only the first of a succession of ecclesiastical assaults against the preferential option for the poor proposed by the Medellin Conference.

Mario did me a great favour by introducing me to his friends, Chilean priests, religious brothers and sisters working among the people, completely involved in the resistance to the dictatorship, who lived in different marginal neighbourhoods and worked to support and promote social reorganization, often at the risk of their lives. I came to know Panchita, Blanca, Marie-Denise, Odile, Elena, Juana, Mariano, Roberto, Pepe, Rafael and many others. These people had a decisive influence on me; they lived the commitment of which I dreamed, and I embarked down the path they had forged.

10
In La Bandera

Building a grassroots Christian community

In February 1977, after a year and a half of acclimatization, it was time for me to start a new project. Along with André Dionne, a companion of mine from the Quebec Foreign Missions Society, I proposed that a grassroots Christian community be developed as an experiment. Instead of entering a new neighbourhood by way of the ministry and the sacraments, we would join the struggles of the residents and work in their own organizations. The proposal was taken up by the diocesan assembly of the southern zone and, after much discussion, we were given the green light to work in La Bandera.[1]

We argued and debated, in very stimulating meetings of the Vicariate of Pastoral Workers, on what approach to take with the base communities. Hundreds of nuns and priests lived in the low-income neighbourhoods of Santiago. My fellow Québécois were assigned to work in pairs in three major districts of the capital. We decided to adopt a simple lifestyle, to integrate ourselves into the neighbourhoods and share the lives and concerns of the people.

---

1. The community was named *La Bandera* (the flag) in honour of the revolutionary red and black flag of the first squatters.

But it was not enough. The burning question arose: would we continue to administer the sacraments *en masse*, to celebrate Mass, to organize catechetical groups, charitable and pastoral activities, while fundamental freedoms were being trashed, people's rights to life and dignity were being threatened, the freedom of association being denied? What did "bring good news to the poor" mean in this context? We were on a mission, but to do what?

Jesus of Nazareth did not organize a church. He went out among the poor, the sick, the marginalized. He placed the downtrodden in the centre of "God's Regime." He was eager to see this "Regime (Kingdom)" come into existence, where everyone would have a place at the table of humanity. He was equally welcoming to his Jewish coreligionists as to the Samaritan heretics or heathen nations, in which he discerned an even greater faith than in Israel. How then, we wondered, could we be faithful to the Gospel message under Pinochet's murderous plan?

A less than triumphant arrival in La Bandera

Towards the end of the summer, during the last week of February, under a burning sun, we began to explore the dusty streets and avenues of the neighbourhood to learn the composition of the four sectors that formed this *población*. Two religious communities of women had already been established. Two Maryknoll sisters, Ita and Carla, had arrived in sector four shortly before the 1973 coup and, more recently, three nuns from a community in Spain had settled in sector two. In each of these sectors, a small wood-planked chapel served to house their catechetical and solidarity activities, and provided a place for prayer.

It only took one visit to realize just how unwelcome we were. In both cases, these courageous women, close to the people, had chosen La Bandera precisely because there were no priests around. They were fed up with always having to submit to the priests and be at the mercy of their often misogynist and arbitrary decisions. For the first time, I heard in the Castilian accent of Consuelo, that we priests, without exception, were macho. She was right, but I didn't realize it yet. I felt confronted by their criticisms of us, naïvely believing they would change their minds once they got to know us a little better. We would just have to be cautious in our approach. These women, with their recriminations and protests, began my conversion to feminism, but I must confess that it did not happen smoothly or without resistance on my part. Our relations with them were strained.

Carla suggested we reach out to a community kitchen that had been organized in sector one. In the back yard of someone's home, a group of women were busy preparing a community meal for the neighbourhood kids. The hostess came to us, surprised to see two young gringos at the door. We made the acquaintance of four mothers, who welcomed us with kindness and good humour. We explained our desire to live in the neighbourhood and support people in their daily lives. As they were about to start cooking, one of them handed us a knife and invited us to peel some potatoes.

"That's it, our daily life."

We were back in a couple of days.

"We'd like to move into the area as soon as possible."

Teasingly, playfully, Juana, a young widow with three small children, jokingly said: "Hmm! Two good-looking gringos like you, I'd take them in, no problem!"

Into the heart of the struggle

Unknowingly, we had landed in the centre of this huge neighbourhood, in the same place where the squat had started on January 25, 1970. The police had dismantled it the same day, but five hundred evicted families were back one day later, having decided to hold their ground and face down the repression. Hundreds of other families had joined them and the group had become organized, with the slogan: “A house or death.” On the same street, right next to the community kitchen, was the home of Victor Toro, the leader of the squat. He was now in prison and would later be deported. These were the people we would be working with, people who had fought for and won, through united struggle, their right to a decent home, and they were very proud. When we arrived, the neighbourhood had about fifty thousand inhabitants.

A few days later, we checked to see if Juana had been serious when she offered us her hospitality. She told us: “They gave me a house with no walls on the inside. Make yourself a bedroom in one of the corners.”

The women’s group went out looking for discarded lumber and pieces of used plywood and the next day, with a couple of armloads of planks, we built ourselves a small room measuring three by three metres. And we had wanted to be discreet! We only needed to get some beds and something to hang our clothes in from a neighbourhood handyman, and we made our triumphant entry, with two suitcases and our pallets, perched on a cart pulled by an old nag driven by an old teamster. We moved our belongings over to Doña Juana’s. It reminded me of how the biblical prophet Elijah, during a drought, took refuge with a poor widow. She shared her last provisions with him. It still moves me today to remember those beginnings in La Bandera. A few weeks later, walking the neighbourhood in search of contacts, we were offered the possibility of a small house with a plot of land. A family, fearing for their safety, was preparing to flee the country. We had finally found shelter in Aurora Alley in Chile!

First beginnings of community

During Holy Week, the Spanish nuns came to ask if we could take in a young man they had known in Copiapó, a city in the north where they had worked.

"We know him very well; he was a catechist in the parish. He was arrested during the coup. He was brutally tortured because he was active in the MIR. We visited him regularly in prison; but he doesn't have any family here in Santiago, and he's very lonely. He's just been released with several other political prisoners. Do you think you could take him in for a while? His life will be in danger if he has nowhere to be."

Reinaldo, who had spent nine months in prison, in solitary confinement most of the time, joined our project. In addition to being tortured, he had also been taken out to the desert for a mock execution. Of all his fellow party members, he was the only one not to have been shot, because, probably, he was still a minor when he was arrested.

Reinaldo was the Chilean we needed for our team. Christian and revolutionary, he arrived in a state of great stress and filled with a deep anger. He immediately got involved. Pilar, a young single woman who lived with her sister's family and was the national leader of the Young Catholic Workers, also joined us. For over a year, our small team met weekly around the table to discuss the situation in the area and to celebrate a Mass of the catacombs. This period seemed to never end for those of us who wanted to change the world, because we felt completely useless. The people had seen so much repression that they were terrorized and distrustful. Their leaders were in prison, missing or dead, and any past political or trade union activity had become a crime under the dictatorship. The arrival of two gringos aroused suspicion: "Where do they come from? Are they CIA?" We wanted to get involved in grassroots organizations, but they had been outlawed and had ceased to exist since the coup.

The challenge of fitting in

The nuns came often to the neighbourhood. They'd spend the afternoon in one of the women's homes, talking with them and sharing their work. They were therefore pretty in touch with the reality of the women's lives. They encouraged us to do the same, but, being young, foreign, single men, it was out of the question for us to visit women in their homes alone while their husbands were at work. In such a macho world, we'd be stepping right in it. What did the neighbourhood men do? They went to work during the day, if they could find it. We had to look for work too.

Our neighbour, Wence, was unemployed at the time and thoroughly discouraged. His wife Marta worked as a wealthy family's maid for a pittance; she had recently become pregnant. The couple's three teens were in an advanced state of malnutrition and were forced to get their meals at one of the community kitchens. Wence had opened a small shoe repair stall to bring in a few pesos. I asked if I could lend a hand. This would enable me to learn the shoemaker's trade. But my new job was short-lived. He soon closed up shop, happy to finally get a steady job as a janitor.

The social crisis had reached terrible proportions; the unemployment rate was sky high in our neighbourhood, and people were forced to survive on their wits. The dictatorship had set up a social program for the unemployed: the minimum employment program, which provided unnecessary and demeaning community work in exchange for a paltry monthly amount, not even enough to provide the daily bread. We saw groups of men and women everywhere, brooms in hand, sweeping up the dust from our dirt roads.

A well-rounded and thoughtful social education

Chile had well-educated professionals, some of whom joined the resistance. We were fortunate to be able to count on specialists in sociology, economics, law and politics, who taught us about human rights, national security and neoliberal ideology, which was getting its first field test in Chile. It was possible for us to analyse the first major economic reforms of the Chicago Boys, the Chilean market economists trained by Milton Friedman, who returned home to assume positions of leadership after the coup. These educational meetings, organized by the Vicariate of Pastoral Workers, gave us a better understanding of the rationale behind the dictatorship and the social project that underlay all the horrors we were being subjected to. The Belgian priest, Joseph Comblin, a sociologist and a great teacher, was then a beacon for those who wanted to understand what was happening, in particular, the National Security Doctrine. According to this ideology, the national army had to declare war on the internal enemy, communism. In fact, the military led a war against its own people. In Puebla, in 1979, the Latin American Bishops' Conference denounced this alleged doctrine:

> The last few years have seen the growing importance in our continent of the so-called Doctrine of National Security, which is in fact more ideology than doctrine. It is linked to a certain elitist, hierarchical, political and economic model which denies the vast majority of the population any part in political decision-making. In certain Latin American countries it is even justified in terms of defending Western, Christian civilization. It has developed a repressive apparatus to reinforce its concept of 'permanent warfare.' In some cases its intentions are clearly political.[2]

In 1978, the Diocese of Santiago offered me a scholarship to attend a course in Latin American pastoral theology in Caxias do Sul, Brazil. It was a rare opportunity to learn from other people's experiences joining movements for social change and base communities. Participants included Christian activists working in low-income neighbourhoods or rural areas, involved in defending the rights of the poor throughout South America. The courses were given over a period of three months by committed theologians and experts in sociology and anthropology.

2. Puebla Document, no. 547.

My studies helped me turn my intuitions into convictions and set me squarely on my path for years to come. I met the biblical scholar, Carlos Meister, who became my mentor in reading the Bible from the perspective of the poor. Brazil, the first country in the region to come under military dictatorship in 1964, was still living in a climate of serious repression, and the experiences of the Brazilian Church were very valuable to those of us going through something similar.

The wind shifts

In August 1978, Pope Paul VI died of a heart attack. Cardinal Silva summoned us to a funeral Mass at the cathedral, which I made a point of attending. Arriving at the Plaza de Armas in front of the church, I was blocked by hundreds of soldiers guarding the entrance. Everyone was forced to submit to a search and show our credentials. This prelude held the real potential of being deeply disturbing, but I managed to make it inside, grumbling. The nave was crowded and in front, in the choir, facing the Papal Nuncio and the cardinal, stood the four generals of the military junta in full dress uniform: Pinochet, Merino, Leigh and Mendoza. The Mass unfolded, sumptuous and monotonous, with eulogies and all the trimmings. At the moment of communion, the cardinal gave the kiss of peace to Pinochet and the three other torturers who accompanied him. Disgusted by the honour being given to such hypocrites, I quickly left. It was impossible for me to tolerate such a masquerade.

Upon his return from the conclave where the cardinals had elected John Paul I as pope, Cardinal Silva expressed his satisfaction as he descended from the plane: "We've been saved from having a Polish pope," he joked.

He had no idea that just a few weeks later he would return to Rome to elect Karol Wojtyla, Pope John Paul II. For those of us who were involved with the poor of Latin America, things were about to get a great deal more complicated. John Paul II, who had resisted the communist government as Archbishop of Kracow, was convinced that liberation theology was a tool of the communists to infiltrate the Church. Under his reign, we would experience constant persecution.

The first hunger strike

An important event occurred that would transform our presence in La Bandera. On May 22, 1978, in three parishes of Santiago and at the headquarters of UNICEF, a number of women from the Association of the Families of the Detained and Disappeared (AFDD) began hunger strikes. At first isolated and terrorized, these people, mostly women, had begun looking for a son or a daughter, a spouse or a parent, who had been kidnapped by security forces and whose fate was unknown. At the time, there were an estimated thousand disappearances in the capital alone. The dictatorship brazenly denied the existence of disappeared detainees, claiming that the individuals had fled the country. The families slowly began to organize and by 1976, the Association had grown to number 323 members. Despite the persecution, arrests and beatings, these women were the first to stand up and demand the truth about their loved ones, "Where are they?"

When three churches were occupied, it was as if a bomb had gone off. People came in solidarity to join with the strikers. The press raged against the "subversives" who were just out to give the government a black eye with their baseless claims. The clergy were put on the spot: should they spare the sensitivities of the regime or take a clear stand for the victims and be accused of complicity with the "communists"? The debate was highly emotional because we were deeply moved by the strikers' determination. Many of the nuns and priests decided to join them in solidarity by fasting for seventy-two hours. In the western zone, another group of nuns and priests joined the hunger strike, which lasted seventeen days, after which the cardinal obtained a promise from the dictator that the families would be informed about the whereabouts of their loved ones. But these were nothing but empty words, which Pinochet subsequently refused to honour.

"We are practically in a state of war. In any war, people disappear and no one asks for explanations and no one gives them," growled the general.

The women to the forefront

Fasting for three days in the company of a dozen victims of repression was a moment of grace for me, a real revelation. The hunger-striking women were standing up to the dictatorship. Taking their courage in both hands, they became the mothers of the Chilean people, like Mary standing at the foot of the cross. Thanks to their example, I became even more convinced that solidarity was the only path worth taking.

The Association of the Families of the Detained and Disappeared had a great influence on me; I consider that these women were the source of my inspiration to become involved in this liberation struggle. I was fortunate to meet Ana Gonzalez, one of the founders of the AFDD. In April 1974, agents of the DINA (National Intelligence Directorate) sequestered and disappeared her husband Manuel, her son Luis Emilio and his wife Nalvia who was three months pregnant, all Communist Party activists. Ana miraculously escaped the kidnapping and worked tirelessly for the right to know what had happened to her family. She gradually organized others who were going through the same thing. The actions of these people, among the most affected by the dictatorship, marked the beginning of the Chilean resistance movement. According to the National Truth Commission, there were 28,259 political prisoners, victims of torture, 2,298 persons who had been summarily executed and 1,209 disappeared detainees. These courageous mothers overcame their fears and held up against all odds. In their non-violent and determined struggle they served as a model of clarity and determination.

The women were bold in the face of aggression. One day, in the pedestrian shopping mall on Ahumada street, I saw the police chasing demonstrators and throwing tear gas. A young man picked up a tear gas canister from the ground and, rushing the bus full of *carabineros*, tossed it inside. He was quickly caught and given a sharp volley of kicks to the face and beaten with rifle butts and batons, accompanied by a shower of insults and spit. Fifteen of them had their way with him before tossing him like a sack of potatoes back into the police van. He was bleeding profusely. Two well-off women, nicely dressed and wearing high-heels, immediately intervened. Furious at the sight of such brutality, they rushed the *carabineros* with their shoes in their hands, blindly lashing out at the bewildered cops. They managed to pull the young man out of the van but he was immediately recaptured and dragged back in. With no hesitation, the women resumed the battle and managed to gain the release of the prisoner, who took to his heels.

The resistance gets organized

Upon returning home after fasting, a few pounds lighter, I noticed that our relationship with the neighbours had changed. Aware that we were supportive of an illegal and banned group, the people who had been attending our catechetical groups distanced themselves from us, out of fear or bias. We were red priests! On the other hand, some people who were more militant began to visit us, and a new dynamic was established.

In 1978, some three hundred political prisoners who had been previously active in the organizations of the Allende government were released due to international pressure. Gradually, under the radar, these activists worked to reconstitute the left-wing political parties. For us, it had become clear that we were going to do our part to help the people's fight-back by providing a cover of acceptability for their resistance initiatives. The services of the Vicariate of Solidarity were placed at our disposal to make *habeas corpus*[3] applications, when somebody was arrested or kidnapped. Raids and kidnappings by the repressive forces were common. We were asked to hide the persecuted until they could leave the country. Applying for a police permit to hold a meeting in a church or chapel was out of the question. The Catholic Church refused to allow the state to meddle in its affairs, leveraging its status as the official church.

Political prisoners once released were not out of the woods. Not only had they lost their jobs, but they were now listed as subversives, and employers refused to hire them. We helped some of them set up a leather-working shop. I actively participated along with five people; the long hours cutting, sewing, and lacing bags and slippers left room for interesting discussions. Roberto, a leader of the MIR and the workshop organizer, became a collaborator of the Christian resistance. A visual artist, he livened up our publications with powerful graphics and added a dimension to our activities with colourful murals and graffiti. The shop was given a real boost in 1978, when we received a major order: a beautiful embossed leather briefcase was given by the Vicariate of Solidarity to each person invited to the Symposium for Human Rights, convened by Cardinal Silva. But after this windfall, the workshop had to ultimately shut down due to lack of sales.

The community of Holy Innocents

We met a young family from a nearby *callampas* who lived in a *mediagua*:[4] four walls built of rough lumber, a roof of tarred cor-

3. A fundamental legal right that guarantees that a person arrested will be brought quickly before a judge for a ruling on the validity of his arrest. This right was constantly flouted by the Chilean military.

4. A *mediagua* is an emergency shelter, which all too often became a permanent home for thousands of families. Dimensions: three metres by six metres.

rugated cardboard and a dirt floor; the wind whistling through the walls and the water leaking from everywhere, all winter long.

Sergio was among the four thousand people detained in the National Stadium after the coup. He had been unemployed since then and Silvia, his wife, was pregnant. They had a baby boy, Eric, with a great big smile and sad eyes. I can still see this young mother, anxiously thinking in quiet desperation of the fate awaiting her children. That night, while I was preparing to leave their home, Sergio took me aside: "We slept in today; the baby hasn't had a thing to eat."

In this damp, poor hovel, we decided to start a Christian community involved in the resistance. We imagined that the birth of the baby would be a symbol, our inspiration, our mascot.

Marcelita was born on December 28, 1979. Her birth marked the beginning of our base community. On this day, the Catholic liturgy celebrates the Holy Innocents, the children of Bethlehem that Herod massacred after the birth of Jesus. We had found our patron saints: all the innocents that Pinochet's dictatorship had murdered and disappeared. Every year we would remember the carnage while celebrating the birthday of our little girl, nicknamed Libertad, who was growing up in our midst. Our project would be to help our neighbourhood get back on its feet, to defeat terror and to get organized to fight oppression.

In the neighbourhood of La Bandera, hard hit by unemployment, many families had long since ceased paying their electric and water bills. The companies were removing water metres and cutting off the power. Usurious interest charges inflated the bills, even after service was disconnected, and families were being squeezed by the throat. We saw women travelling long distances with a wheelbarrow, carting water with a friend or a relative. Men climbed up the poles to illegally hook up the electricity, risking their lives and their inflammable wooden houses.

A committee was formed to help people in debt negotiate reasonable payment arrangements and debt relief with the utilities. A police permit was necessary for any meeting of three or more persons, and all organizations were banned, and we were once again forced to go outside the law. Through word-of-mouth, we called people to a meeting in a large Franciscan church on the edge of the district: the church was filled, people murmured naïvely that the priests were finally going to be able to pay their debts. It was a prodigious moment. Since the coup, five years earlier, people had stopped meeting to discuss their problems, as before. People nervously greeted each other upon arrival. They were holding their unpaid bills. Little by little, despite the military crackdown, a huge organization of debtors was formed; the problem was so widespread that by the end, the companies were forced to forgive all interest and renegotiate the amounts owed so that people could settle over time. This first initiative gave us back our confidence and set the stage for going a little bit further. From there, we started to set up small committees for the defense of individual and collective rights. These organizational beginnings enabled us to overcome fear.

The kilns of Lonquén

In November 1978, just after the Symposium for Human Rights, an anonymous call informed the Vicariate of Solidarity that corpses had been discovered in an abandoned lime kiln in Lonquén, a small town south of Santiago. In 1973, fifteen farmers between seventeen and fifty-one years of age had been arrested and executed. Their bodies were thrown into the chimney of a disused lime kiln and covered with cement. For the first time, we learned the fate of some of the disappeared detainees. One year after the identification of the bodies by the Institute of Forensic Medicine and after the investigation had reached its conclusion, the families demanded that the remains of their relatives be handed over to them for burial. A military judge issued an order and the families, along with thousands of supporters, waited throughout the day in the Church of the Recoleta, north of the capital. Around four o'clock in the afternoon, we were informed that the remains had been secretly removed the previous night. They had been buried in a common grave, the bones deliberately mixed and dispersed. A howl of pain and anger echoed from the crowd to the nave. Not only were they taking the living, now they were disappearing the dead! The regime wanted to ensure that there would be no demonstration on the occasion of the transfer of the victims' remains to the cemetery. The cruelty was absolute.

In the church, we were all beside ourselves. Then Cristian Precht, the episcopal Vicar of Solidarity, went up to the front and delivered a pious speech to the victims' families about the need to forgive. He wanted to appease the more than legitimate anger of the people that was being expressed. As if it were the role of the Church to stand between the dictatorship and the oppressed people to prevent social violence! As if the growing violence of the dictatorship did not deserve to be courageously denounced!

During my theological studies, I had learned in the Summa Theologica of St. Thomas Aquinas that forgiveness requires three conditions: to regret the harm done, to make amends and to have the firm intention to not do it again. Pinochet received communion in public; he killed and tortured, he caused immense harm and justified his actions by claiming the defense of Christian civilization. It was immoral to ask for forgiveness and talk about reconciliation under such conditions.

After these events, indignation was at its height, and to act in solidarity with the Association of the Families of the Detained and Disappeared, we called on nuns, priests and theology students to fast for seventy-two hours at Fathers of Holy Cross college in Andacollo. There was an enthusiastic response, and several hundred people participated in the solidarity action, including the auxiliary Bishop of Santiago, Enrique Alvear, a pastor revered for his spirit of solidarity.

During the fast, a dozen missionaries from Quebec decided to confront the Canadian Ambassador. Working among the poor, we were shocked by his attitude. After the coup, the embassy had taken in many people and helped them to flee to Canada. Clearly, Canadian policy had recently changed. The new ambassador had barricaded the embassy, cutting off access, and applicants for refugee status had to line up in the downtown street, under the watchful eyes of the *carabineros*. In fact, the diplomat had been mandated to reestablish good relations with the regime and resume doing business with Chile, especially the mining sector. During the previous week, two peasants on the run had managed to gain access to the grounds of the ambassador's residence and demanded political asylum. The ambassador, panicked, called the authorities and handed the two men over to the CNI (National Information Center), renowned for torturing prisoners. Confronted with our criticism, the diplomat was furious: "I had no way to know whether or not these people were terrorists."

"Mr. Ambassador," I asked, "where did you learn your trade? If you are unable to cope with stress, you're not the man for the job. We're going to ask the Parliament of Canada for your dismissal."

This was done, in a letter formally addressed to the government of Joe Clark and the Liberal opposition led by Pierre Elliott Trudeau.

The fast in solidarity with the disappeared detainees had a big impact: there was concern in the religious communities that the young aspirants had participated without the permission of their superiors. The sizable presence of students from the theology faculty at the Catholic University set a precedent that later on opened the door for organizing resistance in this ideological fortress of the dictatorship.

That's what Chile was like in the first years I spent there. I was proud to live in solidarity with the people who were passing through this long night. For the first time, I felt like I was where I belonged, even if any number of insecurities and doubts assailed me. The Church of Santiago played an important role as an institution and the cardinal steered the boat with a steady hand and a spirit of solidarity, while keeping his promise not to break with the dictator. After four intense years, I was entitled to a two-month vacation with my family, but I was already anticipating taking my commitment one step further upon my return. It seemed to me that it was necessary to continue the work our Christian communities were doing in support of resistance organizations, but if we didn't want this ordeal to drag on for another hundred years, we were going to have to actively help to consolidate the resistance movement. I wanted to be part of it.

“Christ is crucified in the working class.” (Good Friday procession)

In La Bandera in 1980.

Sharing a meal with friends in La Pincoya.

With Sergio Muñoz and Sylvia Cariz, who were involved in founding the Ita and Carla Base Community; here we are baptizing Marcelita, our mascot.

Ita Ford and Carla Piette who inspired the Ita and Carla Community in La Bandera

Ita Ford was a Maryknoll Sister who worked in La Bandera, Santiago, and then in El Salvador where the army sequestered, raped and murdered her. "Christ invites us not to fear persecution, because anybody committed to the poor must be prepared to face the same fate as the poor."

Carla Piette, a Maryknoll Sister, worked for several years in La Bandera before answering the call of Archbishop Romero to work in El Salvador. She died in an accident while aiding a refugee.

11

A Dictatorship Serving Big Capital

The Chicago Boys

The military coup in Chile was the first phase of a strategy whose ultimate scope extended far beyond the borders of this small country. The strategy called for the implementation of a new economic model, years in the planning by global business elites, under the leadership of the United States. Chile would serve as the field test, with the prerequisite being a government able to impose a new set of rules. Hence Henry Kissinger's involvement and firm support for the coup against Allende in 1973.

Between 1957 and 1970, over a hundred economics students from the Catholic University of Chile were sent to study at the University of Chicago, under an agreement sponsored by Chilean businessmen. Under the leadership of Milton Friedman, the university had become the most influential neoliberal academic centre. The Chilean economists, nicknamed the Chicago Boys, held the reins of economic power during the years of the dictatorship, and continue to do so up to the present day.[1] Their vision, which survived beyond the military dictatorship, was the dominance of capital over all else.

---

1. These data are taken from the article by Jorge Vergara Estévez, "El mito de las privatizaciones en Chile," *Polis*, 12 (2005).

The savage repression had as its aim the imposition by force of a favourable model for the Chilean economic elites. The Chilean experience demonstrated that the purchase of publicly-owned companies in other countries could be an excellent business opportunity. Multinational corporations began to buy up state enterprises in many countries around the world, with the complicity of the IMF (International Monetary Fund).

Chile, which ranked among the world's leading producers of copper, had a large working class and a strong manufacturing base. Trade unionism was strong in Chile, forged for decades by hard-fought struggles led by the Communist Party. Under the governments of the Christian Democrats and the Allende Socialists, a powerful movement for social justice had emerged: land occupations by the homeless, neighbourhood committees, and farmers' organizations and Mapuche indigenous movements.[2] These grassroots movements, coordinated and supported by the progressive political parties, would be ruthlessly dismantled by the repressive regime.

The regime's opening salvo was to hamstring the workers by severely limiting freedom of association. Next, import tariffs, which had served to protect locally-produced goods, were lowered. Within a couple of years, Chilean manufacturing fell victim to dumping, mainly from Taiwan. This threw thousands of workers in the large cities into unemployment. The third stage of the strategy was the sell-off to the private sector of state-owned companies, which were acquired at a discount by Chilean industrialists and the military. Agricultural and industrial production companies, water and electrical utilities, public transport, old-

2. These Amerindian communities in the south-central zone of Chile resisted the Incas and the Spanish conquistadors. They were crushed by the Chilean army in 1882, and an effort was made to assimilate them. They are still victims of harassment today, and defending their rights falls under the Terrorism Act. The Chilean government does not recognize the existence of a Mapuche Nation on the Chilean territory.

age pensions and social security, health and education; all were privatized. The state was the big loser in the no-holds-barred transformation of the economy, while skyrocketing rates for basic services put the population in a strangle hold. At the same time, the elites happily lined their pockets by looting the common good.

The biggest blow to the economy was the privatization of copper, which had been nationalized under Allende. Copper was Chile's principal non-renewable resource and the largest source of state revenue. Of the country's total reserves, sixty-three percent were divested to Exxon and other multinationals at bargain-basement prices. The state held on to thirty-seven percent of production. Since then, these companies have never paid taxes, claiming losses year after year. So far, the Chilean government has not demanded the payment of any royalties and has turned the country's resources over to the multinationals for virtually a pittance!

The duty to resist

> It is in rebellion that the soul is revealed
>
> To rebel is a visceral attitude, a human seismic movement that emerges from the depths of the soul. When someone rebels, he does it with his guts and at times against all reason or convenience.
>
> Josep Castelló[3]

There was no choice but to resist the military and economic offensive underway against a terrorized people. For Pinochet, it was an all out war against the "enemies of the fatherland," that is to say, the opposition. Over six years, hundreds of people

3. Josep Castelló, "Es en la rebelión donde el alma se revela," published on the website *Escritos de Pep Castelló*, August 23, 2012. [escritosdepepcastello.blogspot.ca] (accessed March 9, 2014).

were forced to seek refuge in various embassies, where they had to stay under difficult conditions until they could receive safe conduct out of the country. Thousands of others fled the country illegally. A few years later, the regime commuted the sentences of political prisoners to banishment, but most of these people were forbidden from returning after completing their sentences. An estimated two hundred thousand people were exiled during this period.

In 1979, the MIR began “Operation Return,” asking its supporters in exile to secretly come back to Chile and help organize resistance to the regime. “They want war, they will have it!” they proclaimed. After several years of decline, the MIR went on the offensive by setting up two armed resistance groups and creating popular resistance militias.

The left-of-centre political parties began clandestinely to reorganize to fight back: the Communist Party, the Socialist Party, the Christian Left Party, the MAPU (United Popular Action Movement), the Christian Democratic Party, the Radical Party. The opposition took shape slowly and painfully, repressed by kidnappings, torture and assassinations, its leadership under constant attack. The Chilean people had to fight on every front and use any and all means against the Chilean army, which was openly in the service of the rich and the ruling junta.

The Christian resistance

I returned from my vacation in Quebec determined to find a way to get involved in the resistance. The circumstances demanded it, in any case. In our pastoral workers group, led by the valiant episcopal Vicar Alfonso Baeza, we discussed the situation of some three hundred base communities in the poor neighbourhoods. These communities were groups organized by ordinary people, believers who were inspired by the image of a liberating Christ. The pastoral workers group analysed, with the

Bible as our guide, what the people were going through, and we tried to figure out what actions could be taken, guided by faith and hope, to transform the situation. The base communities celebrated the life and death of Christ as it was experienced during that time by the Chilean people.[4] This new way of life in the Church had its roots in the "preferential option for the poor." Through the base communities, the poor themselves appropriated the Church.

The organization of Christian activist communities gave the Church hierarchy hives, reminding them of the movement of "Christians for Socialism" which had been part of Allende's victorious electoral strategy—the Popular Unity Party. In La Bandera, we were determined to form this type of activist community engaged in the people's struggles. We wanted to "proclaim the Good News to the poor," but what was the good news that people were eager to hear? In this period where the people had become desperate and had lost their capacity to fight, we needed to help them get back on their feet and rebuild their organizations. They needed to overcome their fears and resume their social and political struggles.

Just back from my vacation, I was contacted by Rafaël Maroto, a worker priest who, for many years, eschewed the status and privileges of his ordination to work in the construction of the subway system. Although he came from an aristocratic family, he had a history of radical involvement on the side of the workers and had joined the MIR, where he played an important ideological role. I gladly accepted his invitation to join the resistance and helped form a resistance cell along with two nuns.

---

4. David Fernández, *La "Iglesia" que resistió a Pinochet*, Ispala: Madrid, 1996, p. 114.

Into the world of the workers

My colleague André Dionne and I had shared with our colleagues from the Quebec Foreign Missions Society our desire to find jobs so we could better understand the plight of the people around us, who broke their backs from morning to night to earn a few pesos to support their families. I became suddenly aware that I knew absolutely nothing about using my hands to make a living. Coming from a family of farmers, André was able to get hired doing agricultural day labour on a piece of land south of the capital, for starvation wages. I headed downtown with the idea of looking for a job in fast food: at least I knew how to make hot dogs! One day, on the spur of the moment as I was walking by Tupahue, a fourteen-storey five-star hotel, I went in and applied for a job as a table waiter or bellhop. Out of the blue, I invented a perfect C.V. for the boss and I was hired as a receptionist. I made sure to keep my status as a priest working among the poor to myself. For six months I worked all three shifts, which allowed me to get to know first-hand the workers' conditions and share their concerns.

The assassination of Oscar Romero in San Salvador

In March 1980, COAPO, which was the coordinating committee for the activist base communities, called us to publicly demonstrate for the first time. Archbishop Oscar Romero had been assassinated during Mass in San Salvador on the previous Monday, and we wanted to honour him one last time in the cathedral. Cardinal Silva sullenly opposed it, saying that Romero was a naïve man who had been manipulated by the Left. This courageous Salvadoran bishop who had been the recipient of numerous death threats and who, every Sunday in his cathedral and on Catholic radio had denounced the killings, torture and horrors committed in his country—this man didn't deserve a Mass? No way! Five hundred of us marched from the Plaza de Armas to the cemetery, with a huge cross emblazoned with Romero's image. We tied bandanas over our mouths to protest the absence of freedom of speech and we softly hummed a freedom song. No chanting, no words. People on the sidewalks looked on, anxious, while a deathly silence hung over the street. The *carabineros* watched us, ready to intervene. What we were doing was illegal. We walked into yard number twenty-nine of the Santiago cemetery, where the mass graves were located. There were many crosses marked NN (no name), which we suspected contained the graves of countless people executed during the coup. We planted Romero's cross in the middle of this field of honour where the victims of the dictatorship were buried, and a brief homily paid tribute to the martyred bishop.

Ita and Carla, martyrs in El Salvador

In our neighbourhood, La Bandera, the integration of the teams of religious brothers and sisters and priests had not been without problems. The Americans, Ita and Carla, shaken by the coup in 1973, wanted a change of scene. They decided to put themselves in the service of Archbishop Oscar Romero, who had sought the help of the Maryknoll community to care for displaced families fleeing the fighting in El Salvador. The two valiant missionaries arrived in San Salvador on the day of the funeral of Monsignor Romero!

They set to work immediately, but five months later, on August 27, Carla was swept away in her jeep by a flash flood and drowned. Ita, who was with her, miraculously survived after being carried several kilometres on the swollen river under a raging torrent. In a letter she had sent to her Chilean friends, Ita wondered what God expected of her in El Salvador. A young woman, bold and playful, an optimist, accommodating and open, she bravely continued her refugee work in a country where danger lurked at every turn. On

December 2, 1980, following a meeting of Maryknoll sisters in Nicaragua, she returned to El Salvador with her mission partner Maura Clarke; two other American missionaries came to pick them up at the airport. Their vehicle was stopped by members of the National Guard. They were taken to an isolated place where they were savagely tortured, raped and murdered by the soldiers.

In Chile, the news exploded like a bomb in La Bandera, where the women had spent ten years of their lives in the service of families of the neighbourhood. We organized a silent candlelight march and crossed the neighbourhood to the Maryknoll Sisters' house. Our community did not yet have a name: it would now be called the "Ita and Carla Community." We who wanted a community committed to the service of the oppressed now had two martyrs of the liberating faith.

The struggle of the homeless gets organized

During the first months of 1980, neighbourhood committees; organizations of women, the unemployed and the homeless; and copper and coal miners' unions began to emerge despite the constant repression.

There were an estimated three hundred thousand homeless families in Santiago. In most cases they were the poorest of the poor: young couples or single mothers with young children who lived in squalid shacks in their parents' backyard or who settled in a neighbour's field, to whom they paid rent for a spot to put up a flimsy structure. The overcrowding led to disputes among neighbours and added stress on many families. After two years of presentations to the mayors and the Ministry of Housing, the homeless came to the conclusion that the authorities had no intention of addressing their situation.

On May 1, International Workers Day, a demonstration in a working-class neighbourhood was organized by trade unions and organizations of the homeless of La Bandera. Our small Christian community took part in it. The march, though harshly suppressed with armoured cars and tear gas, was a positive experience. It took courage to keep on struggling. The next morning, a Sunday, the Church of St. Michael the Archangel on Avenida Grande was occupied by a group of women. I was working that weekend at the Hotel Tupahue. I received a call at the reception desk asking me to report to the parish after work, as the protesters had proposed to Bishop Enrique Alvear that I serve as a mediator. I met with the priest, who was worried that he wouldn't be able to accommodate his parishioners for the Masses. I suggested that he talk with the people inside the church and as he went in, he saw a huge banner they had hung on the front of the building, denouncing the repression of the day before. He turned pale. With the help of Auxiliary Bishop Alvear, a man of the people, we came to an agreement: the protesters could spend the night in the church. We would loan them school uniforms belonging to some of the young college girls who lived in the parish. On Monday morning, the activists melted into the crowd of students at the end of classes and quietly returned home under the noses of the soldiers. There were no arrests.

The squat in La Bandera

I learned that the MIR comrades were preparing to occupy some land. The neighbourhood of La Bandera had been born in the same manner. But now we were subject to war measures and were concerned there could be a massacre. The homeless insisted on squatting and pressured the MIR militants to help them make it happen.

On July 22, in the middle of winter, dozens of rented buses quietly appeared in La Bandera at six o'clock in the morning, discharging hundreds of people onto the municipality's vacant land. It was still dark. The people brought supplies to build shelter: pieces of nylon, canvas, boards, planks, provisions and Chilean flags. In less than an hour, the three hundred and fifty families had set up their makeshift tents, while another two hundred were intercepted by *carabineros* along the way.

At seven in the morning, a messenger knocked on our door and informed us that the army was in the process of dismantling the tents and attacking the families. I rushed to the scene and I saw that all the men had been arrested and taken to the police station. The soldiers were chasing women and beating them. In a state of rage, they destroyed the encampment and set it on fire. A soldier dragged a woman by her hair through the mud and the woman's son, about five, grabbed the soldier by the leg and bit him. The child's courage galvanized my conscience. As I walked, a police van rushed towards me at full speed across the field, to intimidate me. I stood my ground, unflinchingly. The captain yelled at me to identify myself.

"I'm the priest around here. Why are you behaving like this?" I shouted to him.

"They're subversives, you should know."

"Well, you can be sure that the whole world will find out what you are doing here!" I shot back.

Alarmed, some of the women came to me to ask what they should do. The squat had failed, and a number of them had taken refuge in nearby houses. The neighbours, in solidarity, had welcomed them in. The chapel, a modest construction of unfinished planks measuring six metres by twelve metres, opened to accommodate the protesters. The army withdrew and women started emerging from the surrounding homes. I tried to reassure them as best as I could: "Your companions have been arrested, you have to try to get them released. We'll stay here until they get out of prison. Then, you can decide what to do next."

Some neighbours brought food. There were a lot of little babies, and we had to organize ourselves as best as we could. We hooked up a hose to a neighbour's house to bring water to the chapel.

Around seven o'clock in the evening, the last of the detainees arrived with a clamour, anxious to know what had happened to their wives and children. It was a moment of great relief. The decision was taken to continue the occupation of the chapel. People, afraid for their security, asked me to accompany them, because it was naïvely hoped there would be less chance something bad would happen in my presence. The news spread like wildfire to Santiago. The homeless were occupying a chapel in La Bandera!

The camp was set up in an atmosphere of chaos and enthusiasm, with a never-ending supply of management issues. Over the months, workers came to offer small bags of rice, beans, sugar, flower or milk and other staples. A large pot, sent over by one of the community kitchens, simmered over the fire all day: we shared the soup. The cold was intense, and the first night, it froze. The women, and hundreds of babies, slept inside the chapel, while the men camped outside, crowded near the door, huddled around burning tires to stay warm. A guard stood lookout to sound the alarm in case the security forces launched a raid.

The next day, icy torrents of rain fell out of the sky, drenching us to the bone. We waded through the mud. There was no way a thousand people could squeeze onto the property, and we feared for the lives of the small children. The first day was very hard, and the young leaders had their hands full. Late in the afternoon, an army officer asked to speak to me.

"Are you in charge? You've got to clear the place immediately, otherwise we'll do it, and you know, we don't exactly care if you like how we do things. So I'm giving you one hour to make this whole crowd disappear."

He was threatening and seemed determined to intervene. Brother André was there. We agreed that he would stay on the outside to coordinate support in the neighbourhood.

"André, call the cardinal and tell him to come immediately. They're going to attack the chapel."

Cardinal Silva was meeting with his assistants. He immediately contacted the media and came to La Bandera with his team. The television crews appeared at the same time as the bus carrying the special repressive forces. The tension was high, it was dark and raining cats and dogs.

Cardinal Silva was a large man, very warm in the privacy of his friends; in public, he was rather solemn and cold. He arrived, his face tense, his jaw clenched. He did not like priests involved in such a situation. I escorted him into the chapel. The door creaked and a Felliniesque sight met our eyes: in every square foot of space there were women sitting on the floor with babies. There was an overwhelming smell of urine and feces. A wailing clamour emerged from the mass of people: help us! The reverend, moved to tears, spoke encouragingly to the desperate young mothers and promised to support them. The camera caught the cardinal's tears and projected them on to the nightly news and into the nation's homes. They were tears of salvation!

The army was deployed in nearby vacant lots, ready to receive orders. Taking advantage of the presence of church leaders and the media, the organizers of the squat quickly decided to move onto adjacent land belonging to the municipality. In a flash, stakes were driven into the ground around the perimetre and an improvised rope and rebar fence was thrown up in front of the dumbfounded soldiers. We had just doubled our territory. During all this commotion, I learned that a pregnant woman was about to deliver.

"No! Not here, not now, señora, please!"

She came back from the hospital two days later, with little Tomás who was baptized, forthwith, in the middle of the homeless.

"When the baby Jesus was born, there was no room for his bed; he had to be born in a manger. In Chile, when a poor child is born, he is homeless. Every child should be welcomed to this country in a proper home. This will be the poor people's celebration. Carry it on!"

The press release sent out by the homeless to explain their actions was as follows:

> [...] We, the sons and daughters of our country, have occupied this piece of land because we deserve to live under a solid roof, because we are tired of living in miserable little huts. The authorities will surely try to dislodge us by force. We only ask them to remember that we are working families and we have no other weapons than our conviction to fight for justice.

Juan Rojas, the MIR comrade responsible for the organization of the squat, was a friend; I kept a copy of the piece he wrote about the events:

> The existence of a progressive trend committed to the service of the poor—such as liberation theology—and its concrete expression in the person of priests working with the poor, has really helped make possible the involvement of activists in the daily struggles of the masses in the neighbourhoods. This facilitated the organization and implementation of the economic struggle in the poor neighbourhoods.[5]

The Ita and Carla Community hit hard

Two weeks later, on August 8, our companion Pilar was arrested at her family home by masked gunmen who took her away in the dark of the night. She had been with us since our arrival in La Bandera, developing the Young Catholic Workers (YCW) and participating in the Christian community, very much involved working with local women and youth. Pilar was missing for ten days and ten nights, subjected to all kinds of threats by people

5. From the detailed account of Juan Rojas. A few months after the squat, I ran into him by chance at the Ministry of Defense, his hands and feet handcuffed. Later, he was forced into exile in Sweden. [online]. [memoriamir.cl/index.php?option=com_content&view=article&id=130:la-toma-de-terrenos-en-la-bandera& catid=28&Itemid=64] (accessed December 16, 2013).

who specialized in psychological torture designed to manipulate people by fear: fear of physical torture, fear of rape, fear of dying, fear of disappearing. International pressure on the part of Catholic Action in Europe and Canada probably added weight to the demands she be released. She recently told me: "I held onto my pain for over thirty years, in fear of all they had threatened me with. I was finally able to let go, to free myself from all of that. I was only recently able to get back to fully living and to rediscover that I am part of a great divine plan."

There were only about two dozen adults and children who formed the nucleus of our Ita and Carla Community. We were a family, and these events shook us terribly. What impotence to know that one of us had fallen into the hands of the dreaded secret service! Was she still alive? Had she been tortured? Where was she? We had not reached the end of our troubles. For several days, an unmarked car had us under surveillance. My neighbour Marta warned us not to go out into the alley. Another family invited us to share their tent at the squat, which had, in any case, devolved into a total mess. We camped in unbelievably overcrowded conditions.

These were very intense weeks, weeks during which I experienced a visceral proximity to the reality of the worst off in society, under a criminal regime that was doing all in its power to crush them. I, who came from the comfortable world of the North, lived out the untenable and miserable situation of the large Latin American cities.

12

The Dictator Gives Himself a Constitution

Seven years to the day after the coup, on September 11, 1980, Pinochet summoned the country to the polls to approve a constitution in a referendum. All political parties were banned, the prisons were jammed to the gills with prisoners of conscience, no opposition was allowed and there was no electoral list. But let's not get hung up on the details ... we're going to decide democratically! Even I, a foreigner, who was only a permanent resident, I got to vote. And, believe it or not, Pinochet won his plebiscite hands down, with sixty-seven percent voting "yes." The constitution was approved by the military junta, putting the country into the service of private enterprise and formalizing the social exclusion of the majority, right up until a few years ago. Pinochet was inaugurated president for a term of eight years through a "constitutional" process. Long live democracy!

A week before that momentous vote took place, we found ourselves once again in crisis. Sergio, one of the founders of our community, had held some organizing meetings for the squat at his home. One night, six armed men burst into the shack. They searched the place up and down, blindfolded Sergio and hauled him away under the horrified eyes of his wife and two children. Around two in the morning, Silvia banged on our door yelling: "They've kidnapped Sergio! The children are terrified. What should we do?"

As it was the eve of the anniversary of the coup, the regime was on edge and repression had intensified in recent days. Two lawyers working in legal services for the archdiocese were also taken away. The Vicariate of Solidarity denounced the disappearance of the two professionals, but refused to comment on the case of our companion. I invited Auxiliary Bishop Camilo Vial to my home so he could meet with the community. He was visibly embarrassed.

"Monsignor," said Silvia, "you absolutely have to denounce my husband's abduction, the sooner the better. It's the only way to make sure he doesn't disappear forever. You know how things work!"

"But, madam, I do not know your husband; isn't it possible he's involved in politics?"

"We are just simple people, Monsignor; we're not involved in politics. The Christian community has taught us our role as citizens, they've shown us that we must get involved in order to defend our rights and obtain justice. Thanks to our Christian faith, we are committed, and I assure you that as soon as we feel capable, we will get involved in politics. There is nothing immoral in that, on the contrary."

The bishop scolded me for having put his back to the wall and never came back again. With his refusal to denounce the disappearance of our friend, in desperation, we decided to occupy the parish of Recoleta, downtown. Around seven in the evening, we took over the office of the presbytery. The priest came and begged us to stop the sit-in, but we explained to him that it was a matter of life and death and invited him to join us; he declined our invitation.

It was the eve of the referendum. We spent the night in prayer and read in the *Acts of the Apostles* how the Apostle Peter was freed from prison by an angel. In the adjacent church, some two hundred and fifty people, mostly nuns and some priests were holding a vigil for the return to democracy. Silvia and Gabriela decided to go and ask for their support. As of result of their support, the next morning

Radio Chilena spoke out against the disappearance of Sergio, who was subsequently released later that evening. An angel had come.

In November, repression struck again; this time grabbing Hugo Riveros, an artist in his twenties, who had supported the squat through cultural activities. He was arrested and tortured in the Borgoño Street prison by members of the CNI. Even though he had been blindfolded, Hugo was able to get a glimpse of his torturers. During his incarceration, we published a booklet of his drawings in which he expressed the effect produced by torture. The artist's sketchbooks were sold to aid Miriam, his companion, and their little boy.

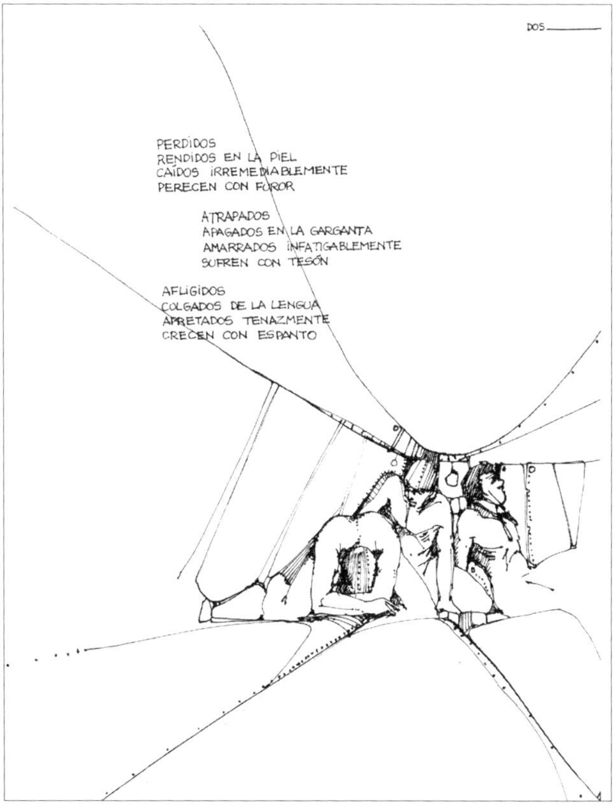

Drawing by Hugo Riveros depicting the effects of torture. (Santiago, Chile, 1980)

Tried by a military tribunal, Hugo was handed a prison sentence, later commuted to exile in Europe. Prior to his departure, he was released and he returned to live with Miriam and their son. He was able to accurately render the site of the secret prison where he had been tortured, and the faces of his torturers. He sent all his drawings out of the country to publicize the regime's crimes, but the CNI intercepted one of the parcels. On July 8, 1981 at two-thirty in the afternoon, Hugo was kidnapped from his home and led away, blindfolded, by four armed men. His body was found the next night high in the Andes, his chest pierced with over thirty stab wounds. He was a danger to national security!

I will never forget the contorted face of Hugo's corpse, his expression imprinted by the horrible torture he had endured. His funeral was held in the church of Nuestra Señora de la Merced, where Hugo had painted an immense canvas of the Virgin Mary, now forever unfinished. Bishop Jorge Hourton, a personal friend of the artist, celebrated Mass with six priests. We wanted to carry his remains to the cemetery, but the *carabineros* attacked us on the square, violently grabbed the coffin, quickly shoved it into a patrol van, and scampered off. I jumped into a taxi, still wearing my alb, and asked the driver to follow the van. Arriving at the cemetery, I rushed up to the coffin and demanded to be allowed to recite the customary prayers. The *carabineros* left me alone in the chapel with the remains. When some of the marchers arrived in silence, holding roses in their closed fists, we descended into a vault to lay Hugo's remains to rest.

Four walls, ten metres high, in which hundreds of tombs were placed, formed a court which you accessed by climbing down a narrow staircase. It was there Hugo was buried, in the family vault. As soon as the prayers ended, I saw an old man standing in the middle of the crowd, weeping with rage, his eyes directed upward. Surrounding this pit in which we were huddled, submachine guns pointed at the crowd. Staring at the soldiers, the man suddenly began to sing the *Internationale*, raising his fist at them, accompanied by the emboldened crowd.

Stand up all victims of oppression
For the tyrants fear your might
Don't cling so hard to your possessions
For you have nothing if you have no rights

Let racist ignorance be ended
For respect makes the empires fall
Freedom is merely privilege extended
Unless enjoyed by one and all

So come brothers and sisters
For the struggle carries on
The *Internationale*
Unites the world in song

So comrades come rally
For this is the time and place
The international ideal
Unites the human race[1]

Then everyone silently climbed back up the stairs and left the cemetery. Dignity and courage had prevailed over brute force.

This period was decisive for me. We had to stand together with the people, trapped in a country that had become a gigantic prison and subjected to the dictates of a selfish and cruel ruling class. I had dreamed of taking the side of the poor. It was time for me to walk the walk. We were fully aware of the risks involved, but that was our way of living the Beatitudes of the Gospel: "Stand up, you who hunger and thirst for justice! Stand

1. "The Internationale." The words in the original are from the Chilean New Song Movement band, Quilapayun. In the same spirit, I include here the version by Billy Bragg, with an assist from Pete Seeger, from the 1990 album of the same name—*translator*.

up, you who are persecuted for seeking justice!"[2] This was my *Internationale*!

A Christmas in the manger

1980 was a year of constant struggle; we had learned the hard way to resist, and had paid the price. In October, with the end of the school year approaching, we prepared to celebrate Christmas with the Ita and Carla Community. Our morale was extremely low; our families suffered from chronic unemployment, lack of resources and hunger. How should we celebrate Christmas in the dark night of oppression? What could we offer our children to bring them some happiness? There wasn't a dry face during the celebration, bitter tears streamed down our cheeks. Oscar, ever wise, rallied the gathering.

> "Christmas, it's a family holiday. André and Claude live with us, and we are their family. I propose that we celebrate Christmas together in their home. We'll bring a few pesos to each meeting, whatever we can manage to put aside, and we'll use it to buy what we need to have a real good party. That'll make sure we don't spend the holidays shut away in our misery, alone and bitter."

I'll never forget that Christmas. It warmed our souls at the beginning of summer. On the brazier, two small chickens were roasting, and you could smell the goodness of homemade bread. Potato salad and tomatoes rounded out the menu, plus a jug of red wine and hot chocolate for the kids. The children were treated to a piece of chicken, while the adults stuffed themselves with potatoes. The infectious sound of *cumbias* and *rancheras* turned up high, reverberated throughout the wood floored house and we danced our hearts out all night long. I can still see Irma, with

2. *Gospel of Matthew* 5, 6.10, inspired by the French translation of Andre Chouraqui.

her wavy long hair, dancing non-stop. She had been diagnosed with breast cancer a few weeks earlier, but at Christmas, she held nothing back. One by one, the children fell asleep, all twisted together in our beds. We celebrated Christmas with joy, the joy of poor people who feel united and who keep resisting, in the hope of a new world.

During 1981, the squat of the homeless in our chapel continued, with all its ups and downs. It wasn't easy for these families to live in such crowded conditions, threatened with eviction, without resources, in constant sight of the police and secret "insecurity" services. Finally, after a year of struggle, the people were assigned land owned by the archbishopric in another neighbourhood, where they could begin to build temporary shelters without fear of being removed. The mere fact of having dared to defy the repression and having succeeded at keeping the squat going was a step forward. From then on, the fight-back would intensify and the opposition to the dictatorship would become better organized and more united.

Somewhat shaken by all that had happened, the Ita and Carla Community began to gather once again in the chapel. During the squat, we had been meeting at the Lutheran church, which had welcomed us fraternally. Pilar was having a hard time recovering from her abduction and psychological torture. To help her get through this post-traumatic shock, she was offered a job working with the continental team of Young Catholic Workers in Bogota, Colombia. She spent three years visiting YCW teams throughout the Americas, including Quebec. Her torturers have inhabited her memory all these years, like a demonic possession.

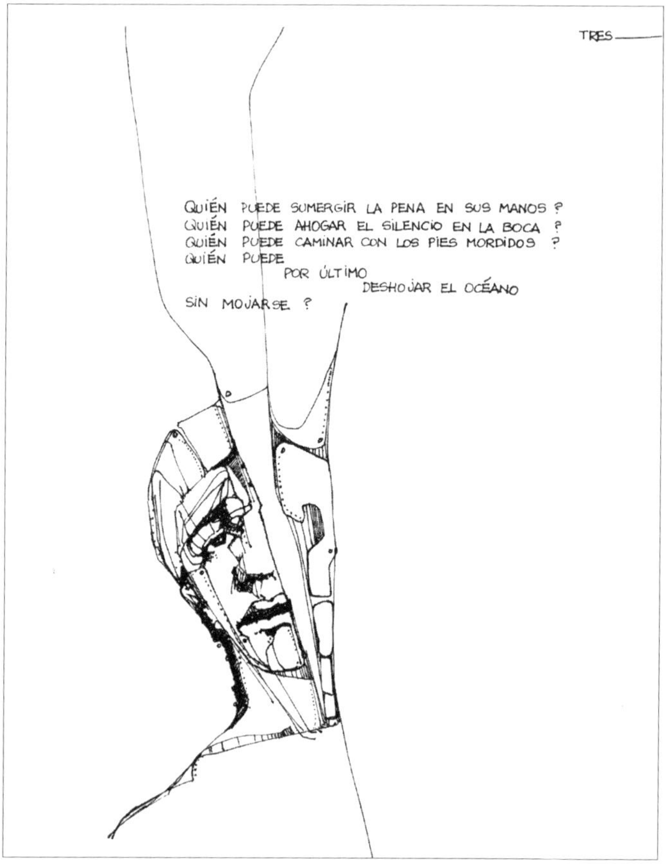

After being freed, Hugo Riveros sent his drawings depicting the effect of torture out of the country to be published. The CNI intercepted them. Hugo was kidnapped from his home by four armed men. His body was found the next night high in the Andes, his chest pierced with over thirty stab wounds. (Santiago, Chile, 1980)

13
A Newsletter for Christians in the Resistance

My work in the resistance was to become focused on the publication of a monthly newsletter that was addressed to Christian communities in the disadvantaged neighbourhoods. The publication was named after Juan Alsina, who was a Spanish/Catalan priest shot by the army during the coup. Juan was a parish Vicar near Santiago and worked in the San Juan de Dios Hospital, where he was a union leader. He was arrested on September 19, 1973. During the evening, they brought him handcuffed to the Bulnes bridge and executed him, throwing his body into the waters of the Mapocho River.

The soldier who shot him in the presence of his captain later gave this testimony:

> We left the Barros Arana[1] by jeep. My captain was driving and I was in the back with Juan. Juan was handcuffed and in a thoughtful mood. He didn't say anything during the journey, and I had no difficulty guarding him. He simply kept silent. He knew we were going to kill him, because they had told him so back at Barros Arana. Arriving at Bulnes Bridge, the Captain braked, and I, as usual when I had to shoot someone, I climbed out, took Juan out of the van and went

1. The Hospital San Juan de Dios, where Juan Alsina worked, is close to the prestigious college Barros Arana, which the military occupied during the coup, using it as a prison camp.

> to blindfold him, but Juan said to me, "Please, kill me with my eyes open, because I want to see you so I can forgive you."[2]

The army claimed that Juan had died in an armed confrontation, delivering the news to the cardinal who did not agree with the worker priests. The prelate, convinced that Juan had been about to leave his vocation, believed the official version and refused to budge, despite numerous interventions by other bishops and priests. He remained steadfastly opposed to the movement of Christians for Socialism, formed during the Allende government, a group the bishops had been quick to condemn a mere two days after the coup, exposing all the members to repression. But never, on any occasion, had the bishops condemned the military coup; rather, they saw the coup as a patriotic action of the army to save democracy!

For Christians working in solidarity with the people, Juan Alsina was a martyr of the Church. His example inspired us greatly during those dark years of the dictatorship. Our newsletter was produced by a cell of four people: we met to plan the next edition, we divided up stories where we would be looking for collaborators. We took stock of the political situation, the activities of the resistance, and we also analysed the positions of our bishops. Deeply involved in this arduous struggle, theological and spiritual reflections kept our faith alive. We were basically trying to bring light to our hard-hit communities living under a regime of terror where information had been totally censored. It was a lot of work, because everything had to be done in the greatest secrecy. During these years, I became a clandestine journalist, having learned on the job.

Once the articles had been received (obviously unsigned), a nun who worked in an office of the archbishopric typed them onto mimeograph stencils. When she was done, I took them to

2. Carlos Gonzalez and Carlos Camus, bishops, *El Padre Juan Alsina, testigo de la Fe y del Perdón*, p. 50.

the print shop of the Disciples of Emmaus; there, I left the twenty stencils with an employee who ran the Gestetner duplicator. During her workday, she surreptitiously printed the stencils and carefully wrapped each ream. I appeared exactly at five past five, just after the business closed, to pick up a heavy box containing ten reams of paper. From there, I headed to the residence of a wealthy woman who lived near downtown. For a few years, she was my bindery assistant, helping me to assemble the publication. The woman, whose brother was an admiral, was proud to participate in the fight against the dictatorship; she hid the copies in her dining room.

She became my friend. She made me snacks, told me about her life, asked me a thousand questions. I made up a story to divert her: I was from Switzerland, married, working for the World Council of Churches in Geneva promoting human rights. I made her call me Eduardo. I spoke to her about my wife and children whom I didn't see much. Until one day, when two young MIR activists asked me to privately celebrate their wedding in the residence of their parents. And my bindery friend turned out to be the groom's aunt. When I was introduced to the family, she burst out laughing. She gave me a wink; I'd been discovered. I never went back to her place.

Once stitched, the newsletters were packed and carefully distributed to the communities, who appreciated each issue and circulated them. It was a way for me to contribute to the political education of the Christians, modeling the link between faith and political commitment. I was determined to humbly continue the heroic educational work done by Christians for Socialism, which had enabled the Latin American Church to establish a fruitful dialogue between Marxism and Christianity and help to build a more just society.

The hierarchy of the Catholic Church had always abhorred Marxism on account of the militant atheism practiced in the countries of Eastern Europe. The Puebla Latin American Bishops'

Conference had warned the communities: "The fear of Marxism prevents many from confronting the oppressive reality of liberal capitalism."[3] But under the reign of John Paul II, protagonist in the fight against communism in Poland, we were made out to be traitors to the Christian faith. The pope strongly opposed the approach of Christians who supported the revolution, particularly in Nicaragua. Indeed, the Sandinista Front had integrated the priests into the government, including Father Miguel d'Escoto, Maryknoll missionary, as Foreign Minister; and Father Ernesto Cardenal, a monk, poet and writer, as Minister of Culture. What John Paul II refused to accept was the fact that the socialist revolution in Nicaragua not only did not persecute the Church, but that the participation of Christian communities had been decisive. "Between Christianity and the revolution there is no contradiction!" When the Pope came to Nicaragua, it was to publicly reprimand Father Ernesto Cardenal, provoking an angry reaction from the crowd. Convinced he was in hostile terrain, he shouted impatiently at the crowd that had come to greet him: "Silencio!" The people of Nicaragua were humiliated by a pope upset by the voice of the oppressed.

A hopeless separation?

I met at that time Julio de Santa Ana, an Uruguayan Methodist theologian who was a member of a joint working group of the World Council of Churches and the Vatican. He studied the relationship between the poor and the Church (taken in its ecumenical sense) during the industrial revolution and the colonial expansion of the West. He had come to the conclusion that the Catholic, Protestant and Orthodox Churches had all worked to relieve the suffering of the poor, victims of global capitalism, by organizing works of charity. But they had never been able to

3. CELAM, Puebla Conference, No. 92.

address the systemic causes that led to poverty and exploitation. They had always declined to question the capitalist system, an act that would have placed the status of their religious institutions at risk. The author asked the following question: "Is there a hopeless separation between the plight of the poor and the churches?"

The publication of the *Juan Alsina, Christians in Resistance* newsletter enabled me to deepen my knowledge of Chilean and international reality, and also to better understand the role the Church of the poor could play in the liberation of a people. It also taught me how to use the media to support the involvement of Christians in the service of justice. Social communication has always been a favoured means of both evangelization and resistance.

In this country at the end of the world, the only way to find out what was happening in Chile was to listen to shortwave radio. Every night at midnight, in perfect Spanish, the endearing voice of the Russian journalist, Katia Olevskaia, reached us from Moscow: *Escucha, Chile!* was our main source of information. With our ears glued to our little transistor radios, we learned what had happened in Chile during the week. Thus, thanks to the comrades of the Chilean Communist Party in exile, we stayed well informed.

14
Demonstrations and Repression

The Good Friday Stations of the Cross processions[1]

I've recounted how we celebrated the martyrdom of the Archbishop of San Salvador during Holy Week of 1980. For more than a decade after that, every Good Friday, the communities in the poor districts organized Stations of the Cross in the streets of Santiago. Armed with placards and banners on which biblical texts were written, the people in procession stopped at places where human rights violations had taken place during the past year. Here, a person had been kidnapped; there, a strike had been bloodily repressed; here, a man had been murdered; there, in that building belonging to the secret police, activists had been tortured. We stopped our march to pray and to remember the passion of Christ experienced in Chile by those who had been persecuted. Every Good Friday, thousands of people marched for three hours, escorted by a busload of *carabineros* poised to intervene. These demonstrations of faith resulted in annoying the authorities, who saw them as a challenge to the status quo,

1. Good Friday, which precedes Easter Sunday, celebrates Jesus's death. The Stations of the Cross is a Catholic devotion, where Christ's passion is commemorated by walking past fourteen stations that evoke different events, in order to be in communion with his suffering.

but who were nevertheless forced to restrain themselves faced with the genuine piety that emanated from the crowd.

A pilgrimage to Mary, mother of the oppressed

At the centre of the great plain of Santiago is a mountain crowned with a sanctuary. A huge statue of Mary overlooks the capital. On December 8, people go there in large numbers to thank heaven for favours received, climbing the stairs on their knees, reciting the Rosary and prayers. On the day of the Feast of the Immaculate Conception, we gathered in the morning by the hundreds, at the foot of Mount San Cristóbal. On large banners each community had inscribed a verse of the Magnificat, a revolutionary song attributed to Mary in the Gospel of Luke. The security services began to get agitated and called in reinforcements. We recited the Rosary and sang hymns. Sergio, from the Ita and Carla Community, had painted an image of Mary on a piece of cardboard: a woman of the people carrying an empty shopping net. Then I heard a *carabinero* talking to his commanding officer on his walkie-talkie:

> "Here they wrote: 'He is looking upon the humiliation of his servant.' On another sign: 'He sends the rich away empty-handed.' Is this politics, Captain? Oh! Another says: 'He casts the mighty from their thrones.' Should we intervene?"

Slowly, escorted by the *carabineros*, we climbed the mountain, stopping on our way. We reread episodes from the life of Mary as told by the Gospels: the birth of her son in marginality, Jesus's arrest, the torture he suffered, his humiliating execution by the authorities. Then a pilgrim, identifying with Mary, shared her own experiences.

> "Mary had no place to give birth to her child. I am a homeless person, I have no roof to protect my family. Mary is my inspiration."

Another:

> "My son was executed by the dictatorship; he was the apple of my eye. He was only eighteen. I ask Mary, who witnessed the execution of her only son, to give me the strength to continue to fight for a fairer world.
>
> "My husband, my son and my daughter were kidnapped, and I never learned what became of them. They've disappeared. Like Mary, I want to stand at the foot of that cross."

In this way, women affected by poverty and violence could testify to their faith and identify with someone usually referred to as a queen, but who was actually a woman of the people, herself humiliated and abused.

We had intended to celebrate Mass in the chapel of the sanctuary when we arrived at the summit, but seeing the militant crowd coming, the priest became frightened, locked the doors and refused us entry, despite our insistence. We decided to hold our gathering in the eucalyptus woods near the chapel. We took a moment to take in the view of the city that stretched out at our feet. At the foot of the mountain we could see the downtown area teeming with cars, bristling with skyscrapers, the seat of financial and political power. And, in the distance, almost invisible, our neighbourhoods on the periphery, concealed in the smog. The poverty belt surrounding the huge city was invisible from the top of the mountain, as it was for those who governed us. Yet this periphery teemed with millions of people languishing in poverty, while the centre dazzled by its wealth. The sanctuary's priest didn't want to let us in to his church. No problem, we'd just take our celebration to the woods!

> "Everybody brought something for a picnic, didn't you? Does one of the mom's have a tablecloth? Great, thank you. Spread it out right here in front of us. Can we share some good homemade bread for communion? And gentlemen, you never go for a walk without a bottle of wine, do you? Everything's taken care of!"

Singing and feasting, we celebrated a Eucharist fellowship to celebrate Mary, a woman like all the women of our people struggling every day so that their families could survive. Something of note, no *carabinero* came to the communion.

The blood flowed all over Latin America

I have already narrated the impact on me of the violent death of Hugo Riveros, on July 8, 1981. Still troubled by this tragedy, we were dismayed to learn that a colleague of the Quebec Foreign Missions Society had just been murdered by the army in Guatemala. Raoul Léger, an Acadian lay missionary from Bouctouche, had been working with Mayan peasants. Guatemala's indigenous peoples have lived in the horror of a war of extermination and genocide that has lasted over thirty-five years. Between 1966 and 1996, over two hundred thousand people had disappeared, eighty-three percent of whom were indigenous. After an initial stay in El Quiché, Raoul had decided to postpone his marriage to his fiancée and to return to join the resistance, well aware that he could lose his life. His body was found in the capital city, riddled with bullets. He had just turned thirty. It was July 25, 1981.

For our Quebec Foreign Missions Society team in Chile, it was both a shock and a realization that we were not the only ones living in horror. In our neighbourhoods, we had held demonstrations in solidarity with the Central American peoples fighting for their political and economic liberation. The Guatemalan martyrs joined our own martyrs. Raoul helped us to discover that not only in his adopted country but also in neighbouring El Salvador, the repression against the peasants was fierce. So our feelings of solidarity extended beyond Chile and spread throughout the continent to the "open veins" in the words of Eduardo Galeano. Brazil, Argentina and Uruguay were also oppressed by repressive military regimes. We were not the only ones resisting. These martyrs were an inspiration.

The death penalty for three political prisoners

In June 1981, Guillermo Rodriguez, the leader of the MIR militias, was captured along with a few other comrades. The rumour was that they were going to be summarily executed in the prison. The human rights organizations demanded that they receive fair trials. The Ita and Carla Community decided to protest by organizing a march to the prison where they were being held. One hundred people marched from the Andacollo church to the prison. In our leaflet calling people to join the march, we sketched a false itinerary for the march, to attempt to waylay the repression. We moved up the street, with our signs proclaiming God's fifth commandment: "Thou shalt not kill!" And "No to the death penalty!" We were about to cross the bridge that overlooks the Pan-American Highway when, from both sides of the bridge, busloads of anti-riot units attacked us. We were trapped. I asked the marchers to kneel and raise their hands to heaven. In front of the *carabineros,* armed with shields and batons, we recited the Lord's Prayer over and over again, which had the effect of confusing our attackers. I went up to the commander of the troop, which was itching for battle. He refused to look at me. I extended my hand. He stood still as a statue.

"Officer, I've learned in Chile that an offered hand is never refused. I'm the organizer of this process. We are conducting a prayer procession for the protection of life."

"What you're doing is called politics."

"Do you see these families with their children; they oppose the death penalty."

"This hasn't been authorized. You have no right to do it."

"All right, we will obey you, but please, take your men away and we will peacefully return to the church we came from. I know you are a man of honour, thank you, Officer."

Blushing with embarrassment, my interlocutor shook my hand with a weak grip and gave the order to let us pass, under the mocking smiles of the soldiers, who thought that their captain had been outwitted by the gringo priest. In the end, thanks to international pressure, the prisoners were spared. However, a few weeks later, Guillermo was poisoned while still in prison; he survived but remains disabled and voiceless to this very day.

Torture destroys both the tortured and the torturer

On July 15, a captain of the *carabineros*, Ingrid Olderock, survived an attack by a militia of the resistance. Olderock taught her colleagues how to torture and trained police dogs to rape women, in a secret place called La Venda Sexy ("Sexy Blindfold (*sic*)"). It is hard to imagine what it means to torture and hard to understand how some human beings can come to do such things. They live, for the most part, a so-called normal life. They have a job called "torturer." After work, they are men and women who go about their business, visiting friends, taking care of their families. They believe they are serving a great cause by eliminating the "cockroaches" in the midst of society.

There is no limit to what people can come up with to inflict pain on someone. The torture was systematic: placing a hood over the victim's head for very long periods and then blindfolding them during interrogations; punching and kicking them; hitting them with rifle butts; forcing them to stand; depriving them of water for days; applying electric shocks to the breasts, penis and anus; threatening their wives and children with torture in the presence of the victim; suspending them by their handcuffed hands; immersion of the victim's head in a bin full of excrement; simulated firing squad with blanks; confinement in a small space where it is impossible to stretch; rape and sexual abuse, and more.

> As applied to those who were detained after the military coup, torture had three fundamental objectives. First, to get information quickly, with the objective of making other arrests and uncovering supposedly subversive activities of leftist political parties. Second,

> to break the prisoner's resistance, thus removing him from the political scene and leaving him unable to join in partisan or opposition activism. And last, to punish the prisoner in revenge for his ideological or party affiliation.[2]

Torture is not specific to the Chilean military regime. With the war on terrorism declared by George W. Bush in 2001, torture has resurfaced. According to Amnesty International:

> In the years since 9/11, the U.S. government has repeatedly violated both international and domestic prohibitions on torture and other cruel, inhuman or degrading treatment in the name of fighting terrorism.[3]

Canadian security officials have handed prisoners over to countries that practice torture to obtain information on citizens. In Afghanistan, Canadian troops transferred their prisoners to Afghan authorities, knowing they would be tortured. In a directive, the Canadian Public Safety Minister Vic Toews wrote that "CSIS [Canadian Security Intelligence Service] can discharge its responsibility to share the most complete information available . . . with relevant authorities, including information based on intelligence provided by foreign agencies that may have been derived from the use of torture or mistreatment."[4] The United States has used torture as a strategic weapon in its effort to dominate Latin America: the School of the Americas, formerly located in Panama and now based in Fort Benning in the United States, has trained generations of Latin American officers and soldiers, among them Roberto D'Aubuisson, assassin of Monsignor Romero; the dictator Hugo Banzer of Bolivia; the Argentine generals who perpetrated

---

2. Report of the Comité de Cooperación para la Paz en Chile, "Political repression in Chile," Chapter II, "Torture," in María Eugenia Rojas, *La represión politica en Chile: los hechos.* Iepala Editorial: Madrid, 1988.
3. Site of Amnesty International [amnestyusa.org/our-work/issues/ torture]. (January 17, 2015)
4. http://news.nationalpost.com/2012/02/07/csis-torture-exceptional-cases/

the 1976 coup; and many of General Pinochet's officers. Many of the school's students were involved in death squads and committed serious human rights violations. The school still operates under the name of the Western Hemisphere Institute for Security Cooperation. It would be wrong to believe that these barbaric practices are the lot of some fanatical dictators, long gone from our world. And above all, it would be wrong to erase from our memories these abominable practices that destroy the souls of those who are victims as well as the humanity of those who practice it.

A trying weekend

On September 11, the Chilean army celebrated its victory against the socialist Allende regime and repression always intensified with the approach of the anniversary. In 1981, a comrade in the underground surreptitiously showed up at my place in the evening to ask for my help. A resistance cell had been surprised by the police in the middle of an action; fleeing, the men had fired on the police van to cover their retreat, and an activist in the car was injured by "friendly fire"; a bullet had pierced his lung and intestine. He needed an emergency operation, but it was out of the question for him to go to the hospital: he would be immediately detained. His life was in danger.

It was a Saturday night and curfew began at midnight so we went in search of someone who could put us in contact with a "trusted" doctor. After a few attempts (you can't use the phone in a such a situation), I returned empty-handed, just before midnight. The next day, Sunday, I set out to look for a doctor who would agree to operate on the wounded man, using hospital equipment, auxiliary staff, and a safe place! We agreed, my contact and I, that we would meet every three hours to take stock of the situation. Overcoming many difficulties, I managed to organize everything: a doctor who was going to slip all the necessary equipment out of the hospital, a nun who was a retired nurse to assist the surgeon, the office of a local charity organization. At four in the afternoon, I arrived at the rendezvous, ready to go.

"Comrade, our companion has just died. What are we going to do with a dead body on the third floor of an apartment building?"

Time was short.

"Wash him, so he'll be clean and reasonably dressed. At 7 p.m., in a neighbourhood such as this, there will be a Mass. Leave your comrade in front of the church door at 6 p.m.; the priest is a stand-up guy, I'm sure he will cope. Write a note to the priest, asking him to give your friend a dignified burial."

The next day, the Jesuit was interviewed on the front page. He will finally learn when he reads this book, who got him into this mess!

A small victory to end the year

The year 1981 ended with a small victory that left a good taste in our mouths. A Spanish priest, a friend whom I had known during my first year in Chile, was expelled from the country along with two lay collaborators. Domingo del Alamo was a dedicated man, cheerful, a great talker, adored by his parishioners. He no doubt indulged in bad-mouthing the dictatorship, a sin we were all guilty of, of course. A deportation order was served on the three Spaniards. A group of priests and nuns immediately organized a protest to overturn the decision. The cardinal, outraged that the regime was meddling in the Church's business, had made an appointment to see Pinochet in the morning to discuss the case. At nine in the morning on the Alameda at rush hour, hundreds of priests and nuns emerged from the subway station in front of the Diego Portales building, headquarters of the military government. We knelt on the monumental staircase facing the main door, and recited the Rosary. On the wide avenue, motorists honked to express their support. We agreed that none of us would speak to the security forces. Our spokesperson was a Chilean nun, veiled, the only person designated to negotiate with the police. We were immediately surrounded: the captain stopped a few feet away from me, in front of a young Quebec colleague, a recent arrival who spoke little Spanish.

"Your name?"

Silence.

"Arrest him!"

Seated on either side of him, another colleague and I grasped him immediately by the arms, determined to force them to arrest all of us. The captain hesitated, yelling, threatening. The spokeswoman slowly approached, with a bit of a mystical look on her face.

"We came in peace, Captain. We just want to pray that the meeting of the cardinal with the president is successful; we hope that Father Domingo remains among us."

"You can't pray here, Sister."

"But the evangelical brethren pray everywhere in the streets and you let them!"

Meanwhile, we recited the Hail Mary over and over again. For two hours, the "good" and "bad" cops took turns, sometimes to placate us, sometimes to threaten us. To detain us signified for them having to deal with a bunch of unhappy foreign ambassadors since the majority of the protestors were foreigners. It was something to think about, given the negative image of the regime around the world. Finally, we ended our devotions by marching to the Vicariate of Solidarity. In front of a crowd of onlookers at the pedestrian shopping mall, we loudly sang the prescient song "Yo te nombro Libertad" composed by Gian Franco Pagliaro, written some years before the military coup in Argentina.

I speak your name, Freedom
I speak your name in everyone's name,
your true name.

I speak your name, and when it gets dark
and no one can see me:
I write your name on my city's walls.

For the caged bird,
for the fish in the tank,
for my friend who is imprisoned
because he said what he thinks.
For the uprooted flowers,
for the crushed grass,
for the cut trees,
for the tortured body:
of my friend who will never sing again
I speak your name, Freedom.[5]

5. "Yo te nombro Libertad" was sung throughout the dictatorship in Chile. ("I Speak Your Name, Freedom," translated by Philip Stinard); accessed at http://archive.ucimc.org/127.0.0.1/newswire/display/29381/index.html.

15
Big Changes in Central America

The year 1982 began with a memorable trip. Early in January, I went to Bogotá, Colombia, to visit our friend Pilar who worked with the international team of Young Catholic Workers. I found her in good spirits, happy to witness the struggles for freedom and democracy that young workers were leading across the continent. She had regained some of her self-assurance, although she remained fragile. The great Chilean outdoors was helping her to recharge her batteries, and she was nothing but solid in her determination.

The revolution in Nicaragua

From there, I went to visit my Nicaraguan colleagues. What a thrill for me, living at the end of the world in the dark ages in Chile, to cross the border into revolutionary Nicaragua! The victory of the Sandinista National Liberation Front in 1979 had put an end to decades of dictatorship and plundering at the hands of the Somoza regime and the people were enthusiastically reorganizing the country with an impressive level of determination. The two Quebec Foreign Missions Society brothers, Henri Coursol and Jean Ménard, were conducting their ministry in the mountains of Estelí, partisan Sandinista country, a very dangerous environment. The United States was financing armed opposition to the government, and confrontations with the

Contras[1] based in neighbouring Honduras were growing. The U.S. was extremely concerned about the victory of the Sandinistas in Nicaragua. There were armed popular rebellions underway in both El Salvador and Guatemala. It was feared that these Central American countries would fall like dominos, one after the other, outside of U.S. control. Honduras was designated the American "aircraft carrier" in the region, a status which included U.S. military bases and free access to U.S. hawks throughout its territory. Today, there are at least thirteen bases controlled and financed by the U.S. in Honduras, which does not prevent it from being the world leader in everyday violence.

The priest in Totogalpa, Henri Coursol, had used his jeep as an ambulance, surreptitiously carrying people wounded—by what had been at the time the Nicaraguan army—to safety outside the combat zones. The two missionaries, along with the bishop of Estelí, supported the peasant revolution. I was struck by the youthful character of the population: leaders, police officers, soldiers, all were very young, with a good command of the issues and determined to defend tooth and nail the changes taking place in favour of their people, a proud people, standing up and mobilized.

During my short stay, I was introduced to Sandinista leaders in Managua, and we discussed the role of Christians in the revolution. Many of the revolution's leaders had attended Catholic schools and had been recruited there to the resistance. I also met a mother who had lost her five sons in the war against Somoza. She bravely continued to work to build a more just country and was the organizer of a Christian base community. A national literacy program had mobilized young students and helped thousands of people to escape from ignorance. I had the opportunity to attend a moving poetry night, where youth from all walks of

1. Refers to counter-revolutionaries opposed to the revolutionary Sandinista government, trained and financed by the Argentine dictatorship and the CIA under the authorization of Democratic President Jimmy Carter.

life, for the first time in their lives, read their compositions in front of an audience. You could sense that there was a veritable resurrection going on in a country where poverty had hitherto been the lot of many. I emerged moved to tears and hopeful that I would one day see Chile living its own dream of freedom.

Mexico in solidarity

From there, I went to Mexico to attend an international meeting of solidarity with the people of El Salvador. The assassination of Archbishop Romero in 1980 and numerous massacres of the population had sparked worldwide outrage. Civil war had raged for ten bloody years, supported by the United States, who generously financed the Salvadoran military. The CIA and American military advisors organized, financed and trained security services whose "routine" operations included torture, arrests, killings of peasants and targeted assassinations. Over seventy-five thousand people were killed over a period of ten years.

The bishop of Cuernavaca, Sergio Méndez Arceo, had organized the solidarity meeting of Latin American revolutionary Christians. There were close to eight hundred delegates from all over gathered in the cathedral. Don Sergio was one of the heralds of liberation theology: shunned by his Mexican colleagues, the bishop promoted social involvement and supported the people's organizations and liberation movements. During the few days that the event lasted, I was able to experience the power of international solidarity. The meeting with Rigoberta Menchú, an indigenous Guatemalan refugee to Mexico and the sole survivor of her large family, was very upsetting. The young woman recounted the horrors of the genocidal war against the Mayan peasants in Guatemala. They were massacred, entire villages were burned, indigenous political and spiritual leaders were kidnapped and executed in order to rip apart the cohesion and solidarity of the Mayan communities. The army and the death squads were responsible for over ninety percent of the two hundred and fifty thousand people killed.[2]

Finally, through a happy coincidence, while at this gathering in Mexico I had the pleasure of meeting Victor Toro, the Chilean leader who had organized the first land occupation in La Bandera. Victor had spent time in Pinochet's prisons, had been tortured severely, and was eventually deported. He greeted me warmly, "Hi, my neighbourhood priest!" I was proud to know this worker—devoted to his people—who had helped to organize a neighbourhood thoroughly mobilized for the struggle.

This trip helped me to truly understand the nature of my commitment; we were confronting a coordinated offensive against the forces of change in Latin America. The national security ideology advocated war against the enemy within, the enemy being the insurgent people. The leadership in Rome and many Catholic bishops lined up on the same side as the United States, accepting the idea that the changes underway were as a result of Marxist infiltration of communities. At the highest reaches of the Vatican, the masters of the law, convinced of possessing the truth, had for more than three decades systematically dismantled the idea of a people's church rooted among the poor of the continent and walking alongside them. There was a kind of meeting of the minds between President Reagan and Pope John Paul II: liberation theology was among the enemies that needed to be destroyed. Wojtyla and Ratzinger had left us naked and exposed to the savage repression of our tyrants and had delivered the shepherdless sheep to the wolves. The Church's history will record that these men were a formidable obstacle to the evangelization of the continent.

---

2. *Guerra civil en Guatemala. Informe de la Comisión para el Esclarecimiento Histórico* (Report of the Comisión para el Esclarecimiento Histórico de la Guerra civil en Guatemala [online]. [marting.stormpages.com/guerragua.htm] (accessed December 17, 2013).

At the Canadian Department of Immigration in Ottawa

Then, back in Canada after my travels in Central America, I went to Ottawa to meet with officials at the Immigration Department to review the cases of political refugees from Chile. The Canadian government then held the view that the situation in Chile had stabilized and that the new constitution passed in 1980 was sufficient to recognize the legitimacy of President Pinochet. In fact, what they wanted was to encourage Canadian firms to invest and to get back to doing business as usual. I presented them with a recent video filmed by the Chilean cultural collective Ictus showing numerous repressive acts of the Chilean police against opponents. The video showed scenes of incredible brutality that made me nauseous every time I watched it. A particularly violent scene showed a *carabinero* scalping a young demonstrator in front of the cathedral with his bayonet. A large piece of his scalp was lying on the ground. I tried to convince the immigration officials of the importance of taking under serious consideration the applications of Chilean refugees since the situation was far from normal. The business community, eager to invest, was singing the praises of the new economic model implemented by the military.

16

The Church in Santiago Moves to the Right

I returned to Chile in late February, 1982. Since the pastoral work in La Bandera returned to 'normal', I had noted that something had changed with the episcopal Vicar. He demanded that I expel Reinaldo from the Ita and Carla Community, saying that he couldn't be both a member of the MIR and the Church.

"I don't know who is a member of the MIR and who is not," I replied, "but I am certain that this young man is a true Christian. Neither you nor I have the right to judge whether someone is a believer. Faith is a gift from God. Our role as pastors is to enter into community with the people God has entrusted to us. I'm not going to expel anyone from the community."

Bishop Camilo replied after a few moments: "La Bandera is a huge neighbourhood. You need to abandon the base community project and organize a real parish with normal sacramental services."

"You are the bishop, it's your decision what you want to do in La Bandera," I said. "Your predecessor supported our base community project in the presence of all the pastoral agents in the area. We are missionaries and we have chosen to work wherever the Church is not established. That's why I'm not a candidate to be a parish priest. It seems that you have a lot of reservations about us, but it's your decision."

"No, no, I like you very much; but I would like to establish a parish."

Slowly but surely, my time was drawing to an end and I would soon have to move on. During the year, my relationship with Camilo continued deteriorating right up until the moment I decided to leave. I had burned my bridges with him, having marched at the head of several public demonstrations where I was openly in the leadership. I was identified as a leftist, which discredited me with him. Right-wing priests had free access to the national television's microphones and cameras to praise the regime; clergy could show their sympathy for the Christian Democrats without incurring the reprimands of their superiors, but collaborating with the left (hanging out with "sinners"), wasn't well regarded.

Move to the north of the capital

In Santiago's northern zone, the Maryknoll priests and a colleague from the Quebec Foreign Missions Society had established a pastoral reflection centre in order to promote liberation theology in the current practices of the local Church. The centre specialized in biblical workshops, grassroots education, women's theology and ecology. My colleague André Drapeau invited me to join their team, which I accepted with relief. I left my little house in La Bandera and moved to the neighbourhood of La Pincoya, situated at the far north of the capital, in March of 1983. André Dionne had already moved and started working in the eastern zone. In La Bandera, we left behind a Christian community cut off from support from the Church. In fact, two priests had been tasked to set up a parish. They were ordered by the bishop to end the Ita and Carla Community, which had suffered from being excluded and mistrusted by the hierarchy. The members were dispersed, and the community became inactive. Then one day, a member of the community named Pinochet (you can't make that up!), called a meeting and more or less told the people:

> "We walked for many years beside Ita and Carla, two nuns who gave us the supreme witness to the truth of our faith by offering their lives in El Salvador. Then we received two Canadian priests, Claude and André, who prepared us to become evangelizers where we live. They gave us the mission to evangelize our neighbourhood. And what did we do? We became discouraged as soon as we were tested. Our reaction must be to resume our service."

And that's how "our" Pinochet revived the community; the members sought dialogue with the parish, agreeing to offer their talents and assigning themselves the task of reminding the people of the parish that social engagement is integral to the mission of the Church.

Cardinal Silva had arrived at the age where he had to submit his resignation to the Holy See. One of his fiercest opponents, a priest named Jorge Medina, was the Pro-Grand Chancellor of the Catholic University. He aspired to the episcopate. A right-winger, follower of the dictatorship, he regularly travelled to Rome to pay court to the cardinals and denounce the alleged acquaintances of Cardinal Silva as "subversives." But when the resignation of the cardinal was accepted, Medina was sidelined. Instead, Rome nominated another conservative who was close to the regime. Juan Francisco Fresno assumed the direction of the Archdiocese of Santiago in May 1983. For the Church of Santiago it was an about face with respect to the option for the poor. Madame Pinochet said on TV, moved: "Our prayers have been answered."

The new religious leader took office in a time of great social tension. He took the initiative of holding secret meetings at the archbishopric between the regime and reformers in the opposition, but excluding the left. The idea was to reconcile the Chilean elites with the eventuality of a return to formal democracy without the mobilization of the population.

As for Medina, he was ordained bishop by John Paul II in St. Peter's in Rome and, after a few years as bishop in Chile, he climbed the highest echelons of the Roman Curia to become cardinal and prefect of the Congregation for Divine Worship. His rapid ecclesiastical ascendancy was a reward to a fervent supporter of the military dictatorship, who said in Chile, in 1990: “The fact that democracy exists does not automatically mean that God would want it to be put into practice.”

17
The Great Days of National Protests

Our struggles taught us that despite the seemingly invincible strength of the totalitarian monster we faced, it was always possible to find a crack through which the light could seep. The challenge was to discover where the system was cracking. The regime began to crumble in 1983, but it never relinquished its iron grip. At the same time, conditions were changing for the Christians in the resistance; we were increasingly marginalized within the Church of Santiago.

On May 11, the first national protest took place. Organized by the Confederation of Copper Workers, it received support from various political, social and grassroots sectors. The government was caught unprepared by the sheer size of the event. The army was deployed, especially in parts of the periphery, and hundreds of people were arrested. A few days later, troops invaded some of the working-class neighbourhoods, searching over five thousand homes and lining up all the males over fourteen years of age in nearby vacant fields. They were held all day, in their underwear, until their identities could be established. The aim of the operation was to sow panic in the population.

The protests, patterned after general strikes of a political nature, demanded the end of the dictatorship with the slogan: "bread, work, justice and freedom." The protests were held every month until 1986. A few days before the event, graffiti appeared on the walls calling for the strike, and leaflets were scattered all over town. The morning of the demonstration, city bus drivers stayed in their garages, for fear of having their tires damaged or their vehicles destroyed by fire. Without transportation, people on the outskirts of the city had a hard time getting to work, or were not able to get in to work at all. Large numbers of students took the day off. Downtown, small spontaneous demonstrations erupted throughout the day, with people playing cat and mouse with the police. On the university campuses, confrontations were more direct, with students blocking roads, stopping traffic and skirmishing with the police. In the late afternoon, workers left work early and immediately after dark, began making their presence felt: banging on pots, building barricades of burning tires, shouting slogans and clashing with the troops who had brought tanks, tear gas, bayonets and helicopters to bear. People were killed during every one of the demonstrations in the working-class neighbourhoods.

In August, the MDP (Popular Democratic Movement) was founded, a coalition of the Communist Party, a sector of the Socialist Party, the MIR and other organizations. The goal was to create a common front with the Democratic Alliance, which itself had already started flirting with the regime. The Christian resistance chose to align itself with the MDP and organized regular meetings between political leaders and pastoral workers in the base communities of Santiago.

However, we wanted to ensure that the base communities didn't become pawns of the political parties. Some members of our communities were activists in a left-wing party and others supported the Christian Democrats. In the grassroots neighbourhoods, the communities all opposed the dictatorship, but with good reason resisted being manipulated by the parties. In our meetings with the MDP, we discussed the upcoming demonstrations and the initiatives we were considering taking. We did not want to be mere spectators of what was happening in the street, we wanted to participate while maintaining our independence. The feeling at these meetings was fraternal and open.

> "Don't attempt to infiltrate our communities; it's counterproductive and demoralizing. We are determined to end the dictatorship, but we want to act according to our own values, in solidarity with the people's movement."

Our episcopal Vicar, Damián Acuña, a priest with a big heart who was close to the people, stayed well-informed of what was happening in the northern zone. We had often called on him to protect the persecuted, to witness violations of human rights, to intervene with the authorities and even to conduct risky rescues of people caught in the machinations of the secret police. In a homily, he said in September 1983:

> "It's unfortunate that recently and after previous protests people came to us for help, because they had been beaten or because their property had been destroyed. We told them, 'You have to make a claim, you have to go to court, you have to put your signature on a formal complaint.' And often the people answered, 'I don't want to do it, I'm afraid.' How many of the injured have seen their wounds become infected, how many people have been beaten and dared not complain? There are even people who have seen a family member murdered who won't file a complaint. Well, we have to say to you, lift up your heads, respect your dignity, be really brave.[1]

During the fourth day of protest, my friend Robert Dufour and I set up a small makeshift clinic in a chapel in La Pincoya to receive the wounded during the clashes. A Christian youth group volunteered to form a stretcher team to transport the wounded and bring them to safety. I had gone to the medical school to meet with the students to inform them about what was going on in the neighbourhoods during the days of protests. The students, who mostly came from well-off families, had never set foot in

1. Translated from the Archives virtuelles du Vicariat de la solidarité de l'archevêché de Santiago, *Chemin de croix de notre peuple*, homélie du père Damián Acuña, septembre 1983 [online]. [archivovicaria.cl/archivos/VS4b4f4713062f4_14012010_132pm.pdf] (accessed December 17, 2013).

the city's periphery. A young woman offered to accompany us for the two days the protest was scheduled to last. The date was August 11 and 12, 1983. I welcomed her to our little house located in the heart of the community at the foot of the Andes. In the late afternoon, we went out to see what was happening. The army had deployed into the main street, and soldiers patrolled with well-fed police dogs, which put the pack of hungry neighbourhood dogs into a state of rage. A canine crisis erupted; even the poor dogs howled out their protest! Early in the evening, a dozen barricades of burning tires were erected, up and down the avenue. The electricity was cut and we were plunged into total darkness. People beat on pots and shouted slogans. The police pursued the fleeing demonstrators in the streets. The area was blanketed with tear gas, soldiers fired into the windows of the houses with slingshots and ball bearings. Small armored vehicles chased the young men down, and a helicopter followed those who escaped with an intense beam of light.

Our team of stretcher-bearers had to be both cunning and bold to get the wounded to the chapel. Our medical intern treated a man who had been wounded by a bayonet. The young Mapuche had a thick black mane of hair, and a wide gaping cut on the top of his head. He screamed in pain and it was virtually impossible to stitch him up through his forest of hair. The soldiers were shooting with pellet guns. The wounded were being brought in with lead in their stomachs, faces, legs; everywhere.

Suddenly, one of our companions signalled us to be quiet, and urged me to look through the cracks between the boards of the chapel. We were surrounded by soldiers, aggressively aiming their guns at us and shouting insults: "Communist priest, mf c*! we know you're hiding subversives. We're coming after you."

For a few long minutes, we remained lying on the ground without moving or breathing, but after a while, our "friends" were gone. Phew! My guardian angel had rediscovered her serenity.

The next morning, I went out to take stock of the damage. The protest had subsided. There were six bodies of young people, all killed with bayonets in our neighbourhood alone. (The overall toll was twenty-nine dead in Santiago during this strike alone.) One of them was a young man I knew well; at sixteen, he was the only breadwinner of his unemployed family, selling aspirin to bus passengers. The young man's mother, accompanied by the young man's friends and neighbourhood women formed the funeral procession. We carried his body to the cemetery along Avenida Recoleta. Robert and I had put on white albs to impose some respect on the security forces. When we passed in front of the barracks of the *carabineros*, the women set the corpse down at the entrance and shouted their rage and their pain to the almost completely invisible police who had taken refuge inside. We marched with great resolve down the street for two hours. When we arrived at the gravesite I was asked to say a prayer:

> "Jesus said, 'unless a grain of wheat falls to the ground and dies, it remains just a grain of wheat; but if it dies, it produces much fruit.' For each one that falls, one hundred will rise."

The police suddenly charged. The crowd dispersed under the riot sticks.

It is in this climate of harsh and bitter struggle that the peoples of Latin America and the Caribbean continue to fight for their political, economic and social liberation. When I see today how the Arab youth of the countries of Northern Africa revolted against dictatorships, confronted by the army and its repression, I feel a great deal of hope that we will one day see the end of this regime of death that the power of the wealthy and the multinationals imposes on all the peoples of the world. The young people of the planet aspire to freedom and are ready to sacrifice their lives so that people can live decently. Another world is possible.

18

The Bible, a Powerful Weapon of Liberation

When I arrived in the northern zone in 1983, Damián, our episcopal Vicar, amiably recommended that I not make too many waves, because I was under surveillance by the archbishopric. I sensed that he wanted to protect me, and I was grateful to him. At the same time, the comrades in the resistance had ordered me to avoid taking the leadership of any public demonstration, to avoid coming under repression and possible expulsion from the country. It was clear I had to withdraw from the spotlight. As a result, I enthusiastically became involved in organizing Bible workshops in area parishes. Inspired by the broad experience of a biblical scholar from Brazil, Carlos Mesters, who had developed a method of re-reading the Bible with base communities, the group I worked with at the pastoral reflection centre decided to offer Bible studies in the northern zone and to help transform, from among the pastoral agents, everyday people into Bible scholars. We thought it was urgent to provide theological training to the women and men who belonged to our communities, so that they would be equipped to defend the preferential option for the poor.

We were overwhelmed with the response; people needed to be solid in their faith to be able to get through this long night. The courses were held in the early evening in the chapel, and people often came to the Bible workshops directly from work.

The groups varied from twenty-five to eighty, and there were sometimes more than one hundred attendees. The sessions extended over five nights, two hours a night. People of all ages came, including many young people.

One evening, I was stationed at the door welcoming people with large bricks made in a huge kiln directly across the street. I greeted everyone as they entered by giving them ... a brick! They were heavy and messy, creating a certain degree of discomfort. Kicking off the evening, I asked the participants to depose their bricks somewhere on their bodies and to take a moment of silence to ask themselves, "What weighs on me the most in life?" Then, I asked them to write, with a piece of chalk, a single word on the brick.

"Now I would like you to come to the front and tell us what word you have written," I said.

They read words like hunger, unemployment, poverty, disease, fear, Pinochet, *carabinero*, prison, etc. The reality of the people was outlined in a few words, and there was a growing emotion in the room. All of a sudden, a very shy señora, María, approached the front, carrying her huge brick with great difficulty. For the first time in her life she was speaking before a group. She showed us her brick, her head bowed: "husband"! The violence of her husband was her heaviest weight. As the people came forward, a pyramid began to take shape, evoking the Egypt of the pharaohs. Gathered around this pile of bricks, we read by candlelight the text that tells the story of Moses: the enslavement of the Hebrews in Egypt, the abuse of the slave drivers, the oppression of a people and a God who listened to them and understood them, a God who delivered them from their oppressors. Followed by songs of freedom and prayers. In summing up the evening, a mother spoke up:

> "I forbade my son to demonstrate. It scares me a lot, so many things can happen! But tonight, I realized that my child can be a Moses. He must do his part for the freedom of our people. Now I am more

> ready to accept him going into the streets, even though I'm scared to death."

In a parish, at the beginning of a class, a man raised his hand: "Father Claude, we know you to be a politicized man. We came here to attend a Bible class, and we respectfully ask that you stick to the Bible."

He was brief and to the point, but with no allusion to reality. I took in his remark and reassured him immediately: "Just so there's no worries, I'll let you choose yourself the texts we'll study. Organize yourselves into five groups and choose a text that you would like to study."

The people began to leaf through the big book that many had never before held in their hands, somewhat lost in the endless pages, covered in tiny words. The man who had spoken up said that his group had chosen a text from the prophet Amos.

> "We kind of stumbled on Amos by chance. I've never heard of him before. That sort of piqued my curiosity. Could you tell us something about him?"

I was grinning from ear to ear. The next day, I broke the workshop into ten groups and each received a chapter of Amos. He is a very radical prophet. A poor peasant, a cowherd, he goes to question the king of Samaria and speaks to him bluntly, denouncing the rich for the profits made on the backs of farmers.

"Read your chapter of Amos," I said, "and then create a short skit in which you have Amos talk as if he lived among us today."

After the break, we shared the sketches and, incidentally, Chileans love to act. We were literally rolling in the aisles: each team had transposed the message of Amos into the country's reality. Everything was there: the dictatorship, the First Lady, the financial sharks. At the end of the evening, I pointed out that we had not talked a lot about God. The man who had started the evening with his question raised his hand and spoke.

> "I didn't think that God was that interested in what we are experiencing. Amos helped me understand that on the contrary, the Lord is very plugged in to our reality and is not indifferent to what happens to us."

The grassroots Bible movement was greatly expanded during this turbulent period; it helped keep up people's hopes that things could change. People who were impoverished and oppressed discovered a God who was on their side. Young people in particular became motivated to get into action. Also, along with my fellow missionaries, I set up "grassroots Bible scholars" workshops for young people from the poor and working-class neighbourhoods. We held ten weekend sessions a year in a retirement home. We presented the history of workers' struggles, peasant and urban Chile, forbidden subjects under the dictatorship. The next day we would discuss the biblical texts, emphasizing that if we talk about a holy story in the Bible, it is simply that the protagonists experienced the events with all the intensity of their faith. Our Chilean history can be just as holy if we know how to find the Breath of God in the events. These courses were very popular and were repeated over several years, with forty to fifty young adults participating. Many of these young men and women subsequently became involved in political parties, taking their places as believers. For them, the Bible had come alive; its stories reflected their own stories. It served as a mirror that enabled us to look at our miserable human reality in the light of faith and help us get back on our feet, on the march. The news of the popularity of these workshops reached ears in high places, who circulated the rumour that I was contributing to corrupting the youth.

One day, in a women's group, we talked about Mary, the Mother of Jesus. The people have a great devotion to the one they refer to as "the Virgin." A national shrine was built in Maipú by the Chilean armed forces, who chose Nuestra Señora del Carmen ("Our Lady of Mount Carmel") as their patron and General-in-

Chief! It is called Carmencita and is depicted as a Spanish Queen with the Infant of Spain in her arms. Adorned with a gold-embroidered coat, crowned with a precious diadem, she overlooks the flags of Chile and at her feet are brave soldiers with their guns, defending the homeland.

"There you have the image of the Virgin that the powerful have given us. Now let's read in the Gospel of Luke, the song she sang when she visited her cousin Elizabeth. As a group, compare the image of Mary in her song and change the image to fit the text of the Bible."

I could hear them laughing. Suddenly, a grandmother shouted:

"We've left her all naked! What are we going to do, now? She says she is a humiliated servant, so we've removed her royal mantle. We know all about humiliated servants! The crown and jewelry, we sold them to finance our community kitchens and feed our children. The guns and these soldiers have no business there either. Jesus was crucified by soldiers. The Virgin says that God will bring down the powerful on their thrones: we can't wait to see it! You know, Claude, we always knew that the Virgin was a woman of the people like us; but our priests have shown her to us as a rich and powerful woman. We're not about to argue with them."

Through reading the Bible with these oppressed people, I rediscovered this wonderful book, a living book, which continues to be written every day in the life of the people: a current book, full of Divine Breath, to change the world. Not a letter that kills, but a Breath that gives life. We are a million miles away from the fundamentalist "endoctrinologues" who take the texts literally and use them to control, alienate and crush people.

I noticed on the same occasion that it is the downtrodden of this world, the voiceless, the excluded and the marginalized who are best equipped to understand the texts. In their eyes, this text comes alive; they grasp the deeper meaning. "I give you praise, Father, Lord of heaven and earth, for although you have hidden these things from the wise and the learned you have revealed them to the childlike."[1] Yes, the Bible has proven to be a dangerous weapon against oppression. This also reminds me of the Mayan communities in Guatemala who keep their Bible buried in the earth, for if the soldiers were to discover a copy in the village, the people would be massacred as subversives. I am convinced that the Church will only be renewed by being in solidarity with the poor of the world and by re-reading the message of Jesus and the prophets in the light of their reality. The Jesuit Guy Paiement, who dedicated his life to serving the impoverished in Quebec, wrote:

> "If one believes that a Breath lifts up our history and millions of consciences, it is essential to participate in it to the best of our abilities. Believers then become so many nomads who share the path of everyone, carrying in their backpacks a hope that surpasses them."[2]

For that, we must get out of the rut in which the Church has been mired since becoming a powerful and wealthy institution, comfortably integrated into a capitalist system whose values and outcomes are absolutely incompatible with the message of the gospels.

1. *Gospel of Luke* 10, 21.
2. Guy Paiement, "Prendre un autre chemin," in *Le Devoir*, December 24, 2008.

This illustration by artist Juan Aquila was a militant statement decorating the wall of our chapel. It is written: “I tell you, my friends, do not be afraid of those who kill the body and after that can do no more.” (Saint Luke, 12)

Community Centre and chapel in Sector 2 of La Bandera.

The Ita and Carla Community a year after it was founded.

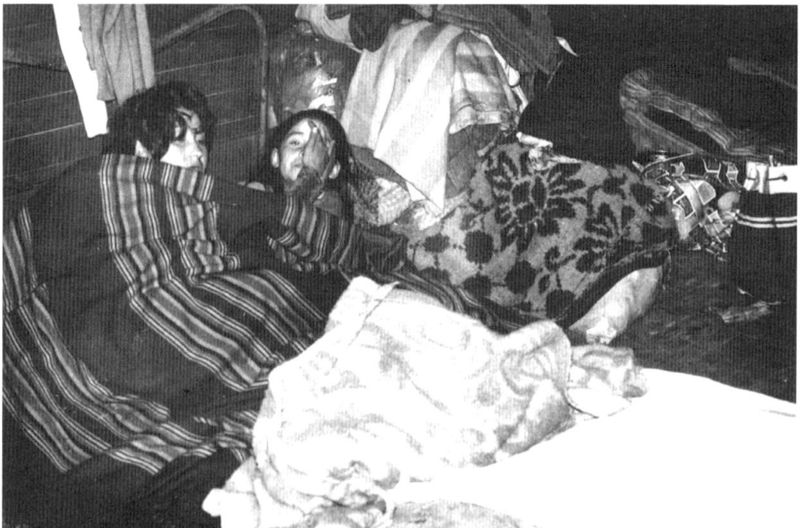

The first night in the La Bandera Chapel during the squat that lasted a whole year.

Preparing the underground Christian Newsletter of the resistance. The mural is of Catalan priest, Joan Alsina, who was assinated by the army in 1973. He was our inspiration.

Pilgrimage to the tomb of martyred priest Joan Alsina in Santiago's metropolitan cemetery.

In 1982, with my friend and brother Jean Ménard, missionary to Nicaragua in front of the cathedral that was destroyed by an earthquake during the Sandinista revolution. The mural shows Sandino who inspired the revolution.

Reunion with two very special friends during my trip to Chile in 2007. Dario Peña was a political prisoner who was freed after spending fifteen years in prison; and Gabriela Ponce, who organized the reunion.

19 Defending Human Rights in a Repressive System

One of the tasks of the resistance that concerned Christians working in the grassroots communities was to assist victims whose rights had been violated, and their families, and to fight against the impunity enjoyed by the aggressors. I have already touched on it, but I would like to delve into the subject more thoroughly, as one of the aspects of bringing the Good News to the poor, that we Christians refer to as evangelism. We never let go of this commitment, and when the great protest demonstrations began, the number of abuses grew dramatically.

The Vicariate of Solidarity

We owe a debt of gratitude to the Santiago Catholic Church, especially to Cardinal Silva Henríquez and his team. With his legal background, he became involved in defending the rights of victims through the creation in 1976 of the Vicariate of Solidarity. An estimated ten thousand people annually received legal assistance to file a writ of habeas corpus when a person was detained or disappeared, or for legal procedures and trial defense. This is not counting the Vicariate's humanitarian initiatives related to food, education and health and other necessities.

The cardinal declared 1978 the Year of Human Rights in Chile, making a commitment to fight so that "every human being has the right to be a person." In November, he convened the International Symposium on Human Rights in the cathedral. Attending were representatives of various Christian denominations and delegates from international organizations. Silva wanted the Catholic Church to serve as an umbrella for opposition political organizations, trade unions and grassroots organizations. In this way, he hoped to show that the Church recognized that freedom of association was denied in Chile. We welcomed onto our premises people who wanted to rebuild their organizations, which had become illegal under the military regime. Without our pastor's firm stance, many of us would not have been able to play an active role in defending human rights. These decisions, although commendable ethically, still were illegal and challenged the military authorities who had prohibited all meetings.

Christians for the rights of the people

In 1980, at the initiative of a group of people involved in defending human rights, the CODEPU (Corporation for the Promotion and Defense of the Rights of the People) was founded. Members of the organization included the worker priest Rafael Maroto and the nun and lawyer Blanca Rengifo, Dr. Manuel Almeyda of the Socialist Party, the former Communist deputy Maria Maluenda and lawyer Fabiola Letelier, whose brother Orlando, former Chancellor under Allende, was assassinated in Washington by the Chilean secret service. Along with these professionals, victims and their families came together to demand accountability and for the return to democracy. It was no longer possible to continue supporting and working with victims without denouncing the aggressors and struggling to end the dictatorship. The work of defending human rights led directly to anti-dictatorship political struggle. It was necessary to support the social and political struggles. From its inception, CODEPU focused on the legal, social and medical defense of political prisoners and victims of torture. Psychiatrist Paz Rojas created an organization for the investigation and treatment of the tortured, concerned with the mental health of people affected by torture as well as that of their relatives.

Over the years, I maintained a close relationship with CODEPU, creating an affiliated group, CRIDEPU (Christians for the Rights of People). Indeed, after the fast we observed in support of the detained/disappeared at the College of Andacollo that I recounted earlier, I kept in touch with the theology students at the Catholic University, who had been enthused by the idea of getting involved in the defense of human rights at the university. Admittedly, the Pontifical Catholic University was the redoubt of the ideologues of the dictatorship and the Right, from which the economical influence of the Chicago Boys disseminated. There weren't very many spaces dedicated to freedom there. At first, the young theologians invited me to lecture on liberation theology in front of small groups. We met in a corner of the daycare, so as not to attract the attention of the police. On occasion, I also met with students in the cafeteria in the midst of the mealtime rush; we pushed a few tables together and discussed the role of Christians in the struggle for democracy. Some students started coming with us to La Pincoya during the protests. They decided to reactivate the university student movement, paralysed since the coup, and to organize resistance activities on campus. Together, we created a group of young Christians who participated in the demonstrations taking place in the capital.

As Christmas approached, it wasn't unusual to see unemployed people trying to earn some money by selling various items on the street. These illegal street vendors could be seen all over the downtown area, to the great displeasure of the merchants, who accused them of unfair competition. The *carabineros* would show up with their police dogs, treating these women and men as criminals. Those who were caught would spend the night in jail, their merchandise and money confiscated by the police. CRIDEPU distributed a leaflet with a picture of the "holy family," showing an unemployed person sitting with his toolbox, pensive and discouraged. At his side, a woman looked skyward, her hungry child tugging at her, begging for a piece of bread. On the back, you could read the Street Vendors' Prayer:

> "Lord, all day I must flee those who pursue me. Dogs surround me to devour me. I am accused of selling things illegally. I am hated because I'm unemployed and trying to survive. My crime, dear God, is to want to feed my family. They will not let me sell, they attack me all day long, their faces deformed by cruelty, they seize my merchandise, they steal my money and throw me in jail. Father, how can I call my murderers my brothers? Bring me justice in honour of your name. Destroy their banks, their financiers, their businesses. Put an end to the looting of our lives. Give us life, dignity, work. Save me from the dogs, Lord!"

This almost literal revision of a psalm from the Bible, distributed by hand, was enthusiastically received. Ten thousand copies were handed out.

CRIDEPU would activate when crimes were committed by the dictatorship; we organized memorial meetings for the victims' relatives. These events paid tribute to those who had paid for their commitment to democracy with their lives. They were attended by Christians in the resistance, as well as by the family and friends of the victim. We read biblical texts that predicted a new world, we sang protest songs, we encouraged people to remain mobilized. For example, when on March 30, 1985 the bodies of three slain Communist leaders were discovered, we organized an ecumenical celebration. Roberto Parada accepted our invitation: his son, José Manuel, one of the victims, worked in the Vicariate of Solidarity and we were very close. In the church, I asked Don Roberto, a great theatre actor, to read a poem from the prophet Isaiah on the advent of universal peace:[1] Roberto, a militant atheist, accepted graciously. With his magnificent voice, he read the text to us with full emotion. In the middle, he stopped short, in tears, and looked at me: "Father, where did you find this? It's so beautiful!"

He resumed speaking with a visceral moral force: the death of José Manuel must not stop us; it was necessary to unite, in unity we would find our strength against the dictatorship.

During these years, CRIDEPU participated in all the large protests, organizing cultural meetings and Bible lessons, and publishing prophecies and newsletters. We published one thousand copies of the Psalms of Ernesto Cardenal, and a book by the Salvadoran theologian Jon Sobrino, *Monsignor Romero, True Prophet*. We were trying to stay true to the ideas and practice of our faith under apocalyptic circumstances.

The Sebastián Acevedo Movement Against Torture

On September 14, 1983, faced with the continued silence of the bishops, still reluctant to denounce torture to avoid offending the government, a group of seventy people met in front of 1470 Borgoño Street in Santiago. They unfurled a large banner on which was written: "HERE THEY TORTURE!" Sitting in the street, the group sang the song *Yo te Nombro, Libertad* (*"I speak your name, Freedom"*). Traffic was disrupted for a moment, and then the group dispersed.

Two months later, on November 11, in front of the cathedral in Concepción, Sebastián Acevedo, a fifty-year-old man whose son and daughter were detained and tortured, set himself on fire. The poor father, desperate for news of his children, died a few hours later, and the photograph of the man in flames spread around the world. The Movement Against Torture decided to honour him by borrowing his name.

1. *Isaiah* 11.

Our Ediciones Joan Alsina published 1000 copies of *Salmos* (Psalms) of Ernesto Cardenal, a Catholic monk, poet, liberation theologian and the Nicaraguan minister of culture from 1979 to 1987. John Paul II publicly scolded Father Cardenal on his visit to Nicaragua in 1983.

Finally, on December 10, after ten years of vacillation, the Episcopal Conference denounced torture in Chile: "Those who in any form realize, promote or collaborate with torture offend gravely against God and human dignity. Therefore, while they do not repent sincerely, torturers, their accomplices, and those who, having the opportunity to stop torture, do not do it, cannot receive Holy Communion." Until then, the Episcopal Conference had limited itself to denouncing abuse. So as to avoid offending the authorities, they had never dared utter the word "torture." Better late than never: it only took them ten years!

Peaceful protests were repeated week after week until 1987, every Friday afternoon and in different places. The *carabineros* and the secret police would show up immediately and sometimes a number of people were arrested; when this happened, the protesters insisted on accompanying the detainees. One day on the vital east-west artery known as the Alameda, the police encircled us and a water truck began violently hosing us down, completely emptying its tank on us while keeping us pinned down. Thoroughly soaked, we piled into crowded buses to head for home, shivering, dripping and laughing uproariously. We found a certain pleasure in thwarting repression. Bystanders, accomplices, we were all smiling.

20

The Army's Dirty War Against its People

I would like to mention here two dramatic events that really shook us up. First, the assassination of the French priest André Jarlan, in La Victoria. It was September 4, 1984, the tenth national day of protest. André had arrived from France a year earlier and worked with Pierre Dubois, a priest who enjoyed great moral authority because of his courageous commitment to his flock in La Victoria. The neighbourhood was very combative, accustomed to fighting for its survival, and the police were unrestrained in their hatred towards its residents.

These two Frenchmen received their inspiration from the worker priests and the Catholic Worker Movement. On the day of the protest, the two pastors worked to collect and treat the injured, to remove the corpses of people who had been killed (there were eight), to try to prevent the tanks from entering the sector and to contain the passions of the residents, keeping them from provoking the soldiers by hurling stones and Molotov cocktails. It was a real battlefield and the confrontations lasted all day. Padre Pierre stood with his arms crossed in front of the armoured cars that led the assault. In the evening, André, a man who was generally calm and quiet, retired to his room on the second floor of the house. He needed to be alone and to rest. When Pierre entered a few minutes later, he found him sitting at his desk, his head resting on his open Bible. A trickle of blood stained the page. He had been shot in the head by a *carabinero* in their wood plank house. On the stained open page could be read this verse from Psalm 130: "Out of the depths I call to you, Lord; Lord, hear my cry!" The funeral was held at the cathedral three days later: tens of thousands of people from the working class neighbourhoods accompanied the coffin, yelling their indignation. CRIPEDU had printed a poster with a photo of André and the slogan: "You will rise again in the struggle of the people." The posters covered the route of the march and the area of the cathedral. This tragic event had the effect of galvanizing Christians in the fight for democracy.[1]

Six months later, repression struck our ranks again and shook us more than the earthquake that struck the capital in March 1985. Two young brothers of a militant Christian family, Rafael and Eduardo Vergara Toledo were shot by the police. On March 29, someone knocked violently at the door of the house of Manuel and Luisa. They rushed to answer it.

"How many children do you have?" asked a policeman.

"Four," answered Luisa, aghast.

"Well, now there are two left!"

A few blocks away, Eduardo and Rafael were lying in their own blood, their backs riddled with bullets. The two young men had recently been forced underground. After that, the Christian couple faced relentless persecution and the sudden forced disintegration of what had previously been a happy family. Ana and Pablo, their other children, were sent into exile to escape death.

---

1. Father Pierre Dubois, a nationalized Chilean from France, was expelled from Chile in 1986. He returned four years later to find his parishioners of La Victoria. He died on September 28, 2012, among the people whom he had defended all his life. Crowds of people from the neighborhoods turned out for his funeral, accompanying his casket to the cathedral. "Father Pierre was amazing, he risked his life, defied the curfew, the state of siege, to save lives," the residents affirmed in a tribute to their parish priest.

Three years later, on November 5, 1988, there was a special news bulletin on television that "two young extremists carrying a bomb had blown themselves up somewhere near the city of Temuco." In fact, Pablo Vergara and his companion Aracelí Romo, having secretly returned to the country, had been arrested and blown up with dynamite at the foot of an electrical tower. The mother of the young woman, Marta, a comrade and a friend who was very dear to me, told me that the police had given her a parcel of human flesh, saying: "These are your daughter's remains!"

I had hidden Aracelí a few years before, when she had tried to flee the country. Luisa, the other mom, began a hunger strike when she learned about the death of Pablo.

> "I don't want to live on my knees before soldiers armed with machine guns. Three days ago, when I learned of the death of my son, I stopped eating. This is my way of expressing my disagreement. My offering, Lord, is this: my son Pablo, my son Eduardo, my son Rafael and all the children of our people, and my own life."

The assassination of the Vergara brothers hit us hard. We knew these young people were not terrorists; they were determined to give their lives to deliver Chile from violence. Can we blame these young people for their determination to defend the lives of their people? The Vergara-Toledo couple wrote in an open letter in 1992:

> "Our beloved children, like everyone who has died struggling against the dictatorship, gave their lives to get rid of a criminal regime and to build a truly united society. All their blood has entered the blood stream of Christ and he begs us to work tirelessly to make Chile a truly progressive country, where we can keep hope and faith alive by building justice."

These criminal acts and outbursts of violence raged until the end of military rule. Everybody who lived through these experiences was left with indelible scars, the reminders of a trauma that permeated every fiber of our soul. Under such circumstances, the bonds of solidarity and commitment that are woven into the fabric of human interactions become eternal, stronger than either death or despair. Our friends and comrades from the struggle became our sisters, brothers and mothers. We will carry them inside us until our dying breath.

21
In the Devil's Lair

"The devil takes orders from Moscow," General Pinochet is said to have remarked. In July 1985, I received an invitation that was to say the least unusual: to participate in the World Festival of Youth and Students, held in the Soviet Union that year. Festivals of Youth had been held since 1947 in intervals of from two to seven years, mostly in socialist countries. The organization of the delegations was entrusted to activists of the youth organizations of communist parties. The festival, dedicated to the themes of peace and friendship, brought together young people from all over the world.

In Chile, the Communist Party acted as an intermediary to the opposition groups to form a delegation of one hundred fifty young people affiliated with various parties: Communists, Left Revolutionaries (MIR), Socialists, Christian Democrats. Ten well-known people from the political and social movements accompanied the delegation. All travel and accommodation costs were covered by the Soviet Union. They had planned to invite one of the Chilean bishops, given the importance of the Catholic Church in the fight for democracy. Of course, neither of them, though sympathetic to the idea, would accept such an offer. Thus, a few days before departure, the MIR informed me that I had been nominated and that I was invited to make the trip. I couldn't refuse such an opportunity to visit the "devil's lair," so maligned by Pinochet, especially since Gorbachev had recently assumed the leadership of the USSR, ushering in the programs of *perestroika* (reconstruction) and *glasnost* (openness), demonstrating his determination to break with Stalinism. Among my fellow missionaries, there was only one I confided in, swearing him to secrecy. The official story was that I was going to visit colleagues in Argentina. For the duration of the trip, I was given the name of Ramiro Ramirez.

It was quite a challenge to take one hundred sixty people to Moscow without arousing the suspicion of the government. I went from Santiago by plane to Mendoza, a city in Argentina located near the border. Much to my surprise, I was greeted at the airport by none other than Aracelí Romo, whom we had hidden some time ago in Santiago! She had taken refuge in Mendoza.

The next day, the Alfonsín government of Argentina, which had restored democracy, placed a train at the delegation's disposal to enable us to get to Buenos Aires. In the airport, I pretty much had to stay on the tarmac. I was travelling as a member of the Chilean delegation under a Canadian passport. The Russian authorities were supposed to issue us visas for air entry that would not appear in the pages of our passports. But one zealous Soviet official stopped me from getting onto the jumbo Aeroflot, because I was not Chilean. The entire delegation was already on board, and the departure was delayed. Roberto Parada came down from the plane to plead my case. Moscow was consulted and eventually it was agreed that I could take the flight, but at my own risk: "You'll have to present yourself to the KGB when you arrive." Finally, I boarded the aircraft, welcomed by thunderous applause. The majority of the Chilean delegation knew me. Thus Ramiro Ramirez became Claude Lacaille once again, for the rest of the trip. The plane was carrying some three hundred and fifty delegates from Brazil, Argentina and Chile, most of them young people who thereupon danced, sang and generally partied throughout the twenty-four-hour flight.

That year, according to official statistics, the festival welcomed twenty-six thousand foreign visitors from one hundred fifty seven countries, joined by some fifty thousand young Soviets. At the opening ceremonies in Lenin Stadium, we were filled with emotions; as at the Olympic games, all the delegations paraded around the stadium with their flags, in a festive atmosphere. I was seated in the stands, close to Gorbachev's private box, with Roberto Parada who was in mourning for his son, slain in Santiago three months earlier. The young activists cordially greeted the delegation from El Salvador, which included young disabled veterans in wheelchairs, on crutches or limping briskly. They had come straight from the hell of war. But the greatest surprise of all was the arrival of our delegation, the last just before that of the host country. No sooner had the Chilean flag appeared, blue, white and red with its star, than the stadium went wild: the Russians jumped onto the field to touch, hug and greet the Chilean delegation. The ovation went on for several minutes, exuberantly expressing the solidarity of the crowd of eighty thousand to the militant youth of Chile, who fought for democracy. What balm, what encouragement, what emotion! To paraphrase René Lévesque, I have never been so proud to be a Chilean. Don Roberto was crying with me; I was completely caught up in his emotion. He confessed to me later that it was the first time he had been able to cry since the gruesome murder of José Manuel, on March 30.

That same evening, on Moscow television news, we learned of the detention in Santiago of the actress Maria Maluenda, Roberto Parada's wife, after a demonstration. Over the following days, Don Roberto and I went for a walk in Gorky Park, and I had the privilege of receiving the confidence of this great patriot with a crushed heart, as he gave free rein to his pain; a person who had been struggling for his people with the same fierce determination for so many years.

We stayed at the Hotel Sputnik, reserved for maximum security delegations. Our hosts had arranged to accommodate guests who lived under difficult situations in their home countries in this high security hotel. The entrances and exits were tightly controlled to prevent the infiltration of suspicious elements. In the hotel, we met members of the Farabundo Marti Liberation Front of El Salvador; the Haitian opposition to Jean-Claude Duvalier; the Iraqi Communist Party, under harsh repression from Saddam Hussein; the Polisario Front, the Western Saharan liberation movement. It was an amazing opportunity to participate in valuable exchanges and manifest the spirit of openness to the world. By accident, my internationalist spirit nearly created a state of panic in an elevator. One day, some Haitians, including the singer Martha Jean-Claude, were conversing in Creole in the elevator and I couldn't resist the temptation to join in the conversation. Stunned to hear a white person speaking their language, they immediately assumed I was a spy, and I could see the look of terror in their eyes. I hastened to reassure them by identifying myself and explaining why I was able to speak Creole.

In the street and on the subway, at the sight of our ID badges, Muscovites approached us with great big smiles: "Chile!" We could feel a great deal of sympathy coming from this very warm people. In the evenings I'd go out with my friend Gustavo, a young poet from Santiago; we liked walking around Red Square. Every night, people gathered around us, asking questions and chatting. I learned to say in Russian that I spoke French, Spanish and English. "*Ya gabariou pa frantsuski, pa spanuski, pa ingliski.*" Inevitably, someone raised his or her hand and offered to serve as interpreter. To my surprise they were very aware of what we were going through! They asked questions about the dictatorship, about Allende, whose memory they cherished, about liberation theology. One evening, more than a hundred people gathered around us in the square, and the conversation went on until midnight. I was a little worried that the KGB would have issues with such a gathering, but nothing happened.

The questions came one after another and people of all ages were enjoying the exchange: there were old Red Army veterans clad in their medals, working men and women, students. I have fond memories of my warm contacts with the Russian people.

I expressed the desire to get a chance to meet the journalist Katya Olevskaya from Radio Moscow, who kept us abreast of the Chilean news every evening on shortwave radio, with her comforting voice on the show *Escucha, Chile*! She greeted me with much affection and spent the whole day with me. She gave me some Tchaikovsky records, invited me to lunch and introduced me to the director of the international radio division. I recorded a good hour of interviews on the situation in Chile, on liberation theology and the role of the Church during the dictatorship. These interviews were broadcast in Chile in small doses, altering my voice so I couldn't be recognized.

I was invited to the home of the Secretary General of the Chilean Communist Party, Luis Corvalán, where I was warmly greeted by his wife and by Volodia Teitelboim, a member of the Central Committee. We sat around the table and discussed our analyses of conditions in Chile. Corvalán knew I was part of the resistance and he invited me to join the Communist Party. "Why don't you work with us? You have clear ideas, you know Marxism. We are the party of the people."

> "Can I speak frankly?" I asked. "You have welcomed me with great kindness, and I would not want to offend you. I've studied the history of the Chilean Communist Party and I read the biography of its founder, Luís Emilio Recabarren. I have tremendous respect and admiration for the contribution of the party to the working class. However, I do not agree with the hegemonic position of the Communist Party. Currently, the Left in Chile is disunited, partly because of the position of the Chilean Communist Party, which has been slow to form a common front with the democratic and grassroots movements. This has led to sectarianism and divisions among the left.

"Certain sectors of the Catholic Church, under the authority of Cardinal Silva, have gone to great lengths to protect the life and integrity of militants, and particularly the Communists. I know you appreciate this solidarity. In the struggle to restore democracy, we've worked together and gotten to know one another. We've established a productive dialogue. However, I know that for your party, this is just a tactical alliance. You do not really believe that the Christians will go all the way through to the construction of a socialist society.

"We are not politicians, and our struggle involves more than just the fall of Pinochet. We have entered into alliance with the dispossessed classes out of ethical and religious convictions, because we believe that the capitalist system, oriented towards greed and self-interest, is unable to achieve the common good of society and the equitable distribution of wealth. We believe in the oneness of humanity, we are internationalists. We believe in democracy of the people by the people, even if experiences so far have been too often perverted by the cult of the personality, the dictatorship of the party and serious repression.

"We fought against communism because it declared itself the enemy of religion, which it described as 'the opium of the people.' I must admit frankly that all too often, Christianity allied itself with the power of kings and emperors, and has long ago lost its innocence. Yes, religion can be an opiate, we have only to look at how President Reagan uses it to justify his imperialist projects. But, my dear comrade, look at the Latin American Church, its fight for social justice and the commitment of its members at all levels to restore peace. Consider Bishop Romero in El Salvador and Bishop Angelelli in Argentina, eliminated because of their solidarity with their peoples; more than one hundred religious brothers, priests and sisters were murdered on the Latin American continent between 1964 and 1985. Think of the participation of Christian communities in the liberation struggles in Central America. These people are consistent with their beliefs and they sacrifice their lives for an inclusive society, inspired by their Christian faith. We will prove to you that we can be consistent to the end. Do not try to infiltrate us to manipulate us; it would be useless and harmful. Let us achieve our mission. Let's be strategic allies, maintaining a dialogue. We are religious people; we have no political ambitions. But we dream of the same utopia, a world of brotherhood, freedom and justice. Let's put aside our dogmas and move forward with the people."

My trip to the Soviet Union was an opportunity to engage in open and fraternal dialogue with Marxists. I had the chance to meet Ernesto Cardenal, a Catholic monk, poet and the Nicaraguan minister of culture. We expressed to him our solidarity with the Sandinista revolution.

It was time to go home. Our pleasurable stay had allowed us to escape the raw winter of Santiago, which was at its height in July. Our delegation returned fortified from our contact with the youth of the whole world who were in struggle, always keeping the faith that another world was possible. It was actually on the way back to Chile that I had the impression I was entering the devil's lair. At the border, the *carabinero* asked me: "Father, have you visited a socialist country, by any chance?"

"Don't even think of it! You should know, sir, that in such countries they kill priests."

He looked at me, as if to say: "Do you take me for a fool?"

And by the smirk on my face, I signified to him, yes. After this short interlude of two weeks, I was ready to get back to work.

22

Even Activists Have Limits

Happy with the smooth running of CRIDEPU, its students competing with each other to see who could be the boldest or most creative, it seemed to me that the future of our grassroots base communities lay in the theological education of the laity. When the repression turned on us, the community needed to be able to defend its options for solidarity with the grassroots movements. So we developed a project called "Gospel Workers." Even before we got going, there were two couples ready to commit as evangelizing missionaries in urban or rural areas. We wanted to provide evangelization workshops to secular people working in grassroots movements who belonged to the oppressed classes. We noticed with what ardor the base communities became involved in the service of their neighbourhoods. Missionaries with a very lively social conscience and a commitment to promote justice and human rights would be able to work wonders. The project was developed by an enthusiastic team and proposed to the Quebec Foreign Missions Society, whose priests were working in the sprawling working-class districts on the outskirts of Santiago. However, we were given a mixed reception, and the project never really got off the ground.

Too much activism

While these projects were simmering, I continued to lead Bible workshops and to train men and women to conduct the workshops themselves. One cannot underestimate the impact this biblical movement had in Chile. We worked under poverty conditions, in cramped and poorly lit quarters, in remote districts, travelling long distances in rickety old buses and without teaching materials other than Bibles, which we bought at bargain prices. I would get home around ten at night and grab a bowl of soup; in winter, often drenched to the bone! Once home, I'd spend some time with Ginés and Ivone, the couple I lived with. In the evening, some local youth would come over to talk and read. I liked this community way of living; simple, full of sharing and brotherhood. It was comforting.

When strangers asked where the priests lived, the residents of La Pincoya would lead them astray and direct them out in the boonies, in case they were agents. I felt loved and protected. Erwin, an eighteen-year-old, hung out at the house. He was very dignified and proud, despite his family's life of hardship. He recycled cattle bones—long known as poor man's ivory—from a nearby slaughterhouse, dried them, and then carved pendants in the shape of doves or made other small items of jewelry that he sold. He didn't have the money to go to school, but his thirst for knowledge was insatiable. He questioned me on a variety of subjects, and I think he read every book in my library. He became a very good friend. Occasionally some friends and I went to relax in the Andes, camping for two days near streams that flowed down from the year-round snow. One day, seeing how exhausted I was, Erwin suggested we go up to the mountains. I had workshops scheduled throughout the weekend. He became angry and spoke sharply to me: "You're about to totally burn out on your work. You need to take a break. You don't pay enough attention to yourself."

He was right. That year—I don't know where I found the energy—the rhythm of my activities accelerated, and I was running on adrenaline. Something was bound to give. I was getting the message that the ecclesiastical authorities were less than pleased. In an ecumenical group where I conducted biblical workshops, it was insinuated that my presence might jeopardize the institution. My workshop co-coordinator, Daniel, was a young Pentecostal pastor whom I considered a brother, and the only one to come to my defense. There was a lot that was left unsaid, and I had no problem imagining the worst. The cardinal was in negotiations with the regime and the right-wing parties to bring an end to the dictatorship and had to prove to Pinochet that he didn't tolerate subversives in the Church. All this represented an additional source of stress.

Melt-down

With my friend Reinaldo and a young couple, we decided to spend February up at the Chillán hot springs, a very popular spot where we enthusiastically set up camp looking forward to some well-earned rejuvenation. The first few days we soaked in the sulfur baths and relaxed in the steam rooms, and hiked the mountain trails. My level of adrenaline fell and suddenly I felt completely drained of all my energy. During the night I started literally bawling. This went on for days. My friends were terrified to see me in such a state, and I was pretty worried myself. After a few days, noting that my condition was not improving, I decided to take a train back to Santiago. Reinaldo accompanied me and located a psychiatrist for me. I went to his office. Opening the door, I saw a man I knew by his nickname, without knowing his real identity: my cell leader in the underground! A physician, he had worked in Angola and returned to Chile to join the struggle against the dictatorship.

After asking about my life and what was happening, he offered his conclusion: "You're not depressed; you're simply releasing a lot of pent-up emotions. You're exhausted and need to rest."

Then, with a teasing smile: "You know, you Christians, you have something very valuable."

"Really? What?"

"Humility! You see, you're a Quebecer, you've received a university education, had a comfortable upbringing, you've been very sheltered, isn't that right? And now you want to become poor like the people in your neighbourhood. Humility is to accept yourself for who you are: a middle-class person from the North who does not have to pretend to be a worker from Chile. Nobody asks you to live just like the locals. Put yourself in their service, be supportive, but give yourself a life. Humility is accepting who you are."

"How long should I rest?"

"That's up to you. Two weeks, two months, two years. Take the time you need."

It must be said that in our priestly training, we had been entrusted the mission of saving the world. A load like that can get to be pretty heavy after a while. My young doctor couldn't have been clearer. "You need to change the way you see yourself and perceive your mission; otherwise you risk burning out all over again."

When Erwin saw me return to La Pincoya in the state I was in, he was saddened. "My friend, I was afraid this was going to happen to you!"

I isolated myself at the downtown central house of the Quebec Foreign Missions Society where there was a room set off from the rest of the house. I spent months sleeping, taking long walks around the city. I wasn't capable of speaking even five minutes with someone; I'd be dripping sweat in no time. I couldn't handle listening to the radio, watching TV or reading a newspaper. I became a zombie, unable to think. The doctor suggested that I take up a sport where I could release some aggression: I chose tennis and worked out two hours a week with a pro who drove me until I dropped. I was hitting the ball so hard that it wouldn't have taken much more to send it to Argentina, over the mountains!

I needed to let off steam. I had heart palpitations, tightness in my chest, insomnia. My doctor wasn't too keen on treating me with drugs. It would all get sorted out with time. I cut my ties and stopped my activities, and avoided listening to the news. In June, I decided to return to my house in La Pincoya with my roommates who would take care of me.

Enough is enough! The departure

On July 2, on the first day of a nation-wide protest, two young people were burnt alive by a military patrol. Carmen Quintana and Rodrigo Rojas were captured while travelling with a group of young people setting up barricades in their district, loaded up with old tires and kerosene. The soldiers doused them with gas and set them on fire, and then carried the two charred bodies to a field outside the district and abandoned them. Though gravely injured, they were able to get help and were taken to the hospital. Before dying, Rodrigo had time to lay charges before a civil judge. Carmen had third degree burns on sixty percent of her body and remained permanently disfigured.[1]

The youth of CRIDEPU asked me if I could preside over the celebration of the funeral. We knew that the soldiers would probably try to stop us, because it was a serious crime and the funeral would draw media attention. At that moment, I realized that I had not recovered at all. I felt absolutely unable to cope with the challenge.

So I returned to our central house with my mind made up to go back to Canada for a rest. I told my doctor, whose face lit up with a smile of satisfaction: "That's the decision that I was hoping for from the beginning."

1. Carmen Quintana suffered second and third degree burns on sixty-two percent of her body. She received extensive medical treatment in Quebec and in Chile. She moved to Montreal with her family in 2010 where she is studying for a doctorate in Psychology.

The day after Rodrigo's funeral, on the evening of September 8, Damián, the episcopal Vicar of the northern zone, arrived with a flourish at our house.

"Claude, you're screwed," he told me, "sorry. I've just left Cardinal Fresno; he asked for my resignation. I refused, protesting that I still enjoyed good health. He beat around the bush for a while and then said, 'Damián, your successor has already been named, and we'll be announcing it on the radio in an hour. It's out of your hands.'"

The old country priest was a good man, passionate. His successor, Antonio Moreno, a fervent admirer of the dictator, had been tasked to bring order to the northern zone! A Bible scholar himself, he hastened to dismantle the workshops organized by the Bible pastoral reflection centre. With the departure of Damian, I was completely exposed; I had lost my protector. I came back to Canada on an extended leave for burnout, without suspecting that I would not return to Chile.

A month later, on September 8, 1986, my friend José Carrasco, a courageous journalist, was arrested at his home during the night. He was taken away, still in pajamas, and when his wife wanted to give him some shoes, the squad leader said: "Where we're taking him, he won't need shoes."

He was carted to the Park Memorial Cemetery, near La Pincoya, where they shot him seven times. The mourning continued, unabated.

Retreated to a cottage in the Laurentian Mountains north of Montreal, I rested and spent my days walking in the woods. A young mama deer had adopted me and faithfully accompanied me in my wanderings with her two fawns. The red leaves littering the forest floor reminded me of all the blood shed during this period. Surrounded by the silence and peace of nature, bolstered by the affection given me by my loyal doe, I slowly began my resurrection.

A time of recovery

Even in Canada, it was hard to cut myself off from what was happening in Chile. The months passed in complete passivity. I spent the winter at my mother's, always a reassuring refuge when storms rattle our lives. By spring I was more energetic and I obtained permission to go to Israel to spend two months discovering the land of the Bible and researching the origins of the tribes of Israel. With André Drapeau, recently returned from Chile, we had a magnificent spring, soaking up the land that had witnessed the birth of the Judeo-Christian faith. I wanted to deepen my knowledge in order to continue re-reading the Bible with the impoverished people of Chile. In June, we went to an international meeting of grassroots biblical scholars in Geneva at the World Council of Churches. In an atmosphere of openness and dialogue, the discussions between people of different Christian denominations from all continents were very stimulating. Sisters and brothers from Korea, Bangladesh, Zimbabwe, Uganda, Egypt, the United States, Chile and Europe had relevant experiences to share about their ways of re-reading the Bible among the people. We discovered that, without necessarily bearing the name, all over the world a theology of liberation was developing among oppressed peoples.

I returned to Canada, my batteries recharged, and hastened to make an appointment with the superior general, to tell him that I was finally ready to return to Chile.

"You're not going back to Chile! It's out of the question. We met with Cardinal Fresno, who requested your withdrawal. You're going to Peru."

My fate had been settled for over a year, but I was the only one who didn't know it. I was just a pawn for them to move around. I demanded an explanation. It was useless; to this day I've never received one. That night, I was awakened by a terrible nightmare; they had sliced open my stomach and ripped out a bloody fetus.

I screamed! My life had just been aborted; I was ripped away from the people I loved. I had never been so wounded as by this authoritarian cleric who claimed to speak in the name of God and who required of me blind obedience. Cardinal Ratzinger's condemnations of liberation theology had infiltrated our missionary society; indeed, around the same time, two brothers involved in the same process of liberation, Éloy Roy of Argentina and Henri Coursol of Nicaragua, were also recalled to Canada.

I had kept a souvenir to remind me of my little house in Chile: a tear gas canister sleeve I found in my yard one evening during the protests. It was inscribed: Made in Canada. Now, I'd be on mission to Montreal. I arrived as an exile torn between two worlds. But during my missions in Quebec, I never stopped travelling to the *Patria Grande* (Great Homeland) of Bolivar,[2] South America and the Caribbean.

It is of this "Patria Grande" that I am a citizen for life.

2. The liberator Simon Bolivar dreamed of the unity of all Spanish-speaking countries; *Patria Grande* is his utopian vision of all the countries of Latin America and the Caribbean united.

23
The Most Difficult Mission is to the North

When the prophet Jonah was sent to the megalopolis of Nineveh, hotbed of corruption and injustice, he couldn't see what he could do to change it. He fled away from his God, and the whale brought him back to do his duty by vomiting him up on the banks of the great city. I was Jonas! Faced with the prospect of conducting my mission in Quebec, I rebelled. My deepest emotional ties, my comrades in the struggle during these years of solidarity, my participation in the biblical movement and liberation theology, I had been cruelly cut off from all of it. Some friends in the Episcopal Church invited me to join their ranks as a priest, and my friend Daniel invited me to teach the Bible to future evangelical pastors in Santiago. But in the Catholic Church, I was caught in an institutional trap.

I reminded myself that in similar situations, it had proved essential to know how to achieve some distance in order to come up with a more viable hypothesis. Apostle Peter's advice to the young people of his communities would help me through the crisis:

> "Bow down, then, before the power of God now, so that he may raise you up in due time. Unload all your burden on to him, since he is concerned about you. Keep sober and alert, because your enemy the devil is on the prowl like a roaring lion, looking for someone to devour. Stand up to him, strong in faith and in the knowledge that

it is the same kind of suffering that the community of your brothers and sisters throughout the world is undergoing."[1]

I needed time to turn myself around, to find my way and heal my wounds. My Jesuit companions fraternally welcomed me under their roof and into their little community in the working class district of Saint-Henri in Montreal; I spent two good years healing.

I had arrived in a country I did not know, Quebec. Since I had left for Haiti in 1965, Quebec society had gone through profound changes: the "Quiet Revolution," opening to the world, support for education and health by the Quebec government, separation of church and state, secularism, not to mention the strong nationalist movement which resulted in a referendum on Quebec independence in 1980. The failure of the referendum provoked a political depression and led to the depoliticization of the population, while a vigorous French-speaking Quebec capitalism, known as Québec, Inc., was stepping up to the plate.

Stunned, I heard from the mouths of Quebec politicians, both in the Parti Québécois and the Liberal Party, the same broken record spun by the Pinochet government: promoting free trade by eliminating tariff barriers, denationalizing state enterprises and selling them to private enterprise, economic globalization. The market economy had become the new faith, the new religion, the new dogma of collective salvation. Everywhere, individualism reigned supreme; it was to be every man for himself. No more utopias, no more social projects. It was the end of history. The birth rate was its lowest ever, and suicides among Quebec youth broke all the sad records.

The challenge of the mission was to confront the globalization of the economy, the root cause of the glaring inequalities: a genuine dictatorship of money. It would either be the God of life or the God of money: we could not serve them both at the same time. It was impossible to get comfortable with this Babylon where

1. Adapted from *First Letter of Peter*, 8-10.

the sole objective was the rapid enrichment of the wealthy at the expense of the billions of people living in inhuman conditions. The Christian North fully deserved Jesus's rebuke to the Church of Laodicea in the Revelation to John:

> "I know your works; I know that you are neither cold nor hot. I wish you were either cold or hot. So, because you are lukewarm, neither hot nor cold, I will spit you out of my mouth. For you say, 'I am rich and affluent and have no need of anything,' and yet do not realize that you are wretched, pitiable, poor, blind, and naked." (*Apocalypse* 3, 14-22.)

What are you still doing here?

One day, some retired professors from the University of Trois-Rivières invited me to talk to them at a luncheon they held once a month. "Can you tell us why you haven't jumped ship?"

Indeed, most of these people had already left the Church and wondered why I myself had not left a boat that was taking on water from all sides.

"It's not as if I haven't been tempted," I replied, "but I stayed because I still adhere to the message of Jesus with all my strength. This is my reason for living."

I am first and foremost a missionary, and also a secular priest. In my previous missions, this status was generally viewed positively by the people that we served. In Chile, for example, where religious practice is at a rather low level, I worked in the grassroots movement alongside many Marxists, with whom we had cordial relations. When our friends in the movement discovered we were in solidarity with the oppressed classes, that was enough to win their acceptance.

"The Padre is on our side!" they would say.

In Quebec, heavy resentment of the Catholic Church and its clergy had resulted in a general feeling of anticlericalism that I encountered every day. I found it challenging. To present yourself as a priest often had the effect of putting up a barrier, if not a wall. After the encyclical of Paul VI in 1968 prohibiting the use of contraceptives for Catholics, the faithful of Quebec began to stay away from their Catholic churches and move away from the Church as an institution. The fall of traditional Catholicism was dramatic, to the point that all that is left are the ruins of a once all-powerful institution. The long reign of Pope John Paul II, who was presented by the media as a kind of a superstar, strived to restore the hegemony of Christianity in the West and to erase the Second Vatican Council from collective memory.

I realized that for those committed to a life of activism, the image projected by the Catholic Church was at odds with their contemporary values. They were ashamed to be identified with such an institution, bringing to mind an image of Christians in the shadows, like Nicodemus who went to see Jesus at night to avoid being seen by his peers.

I remember a meeting with Dom Helder Camara, the humble Brazilian bishop invited to Montreal in 1969 by the progressive Catholic organization Development and Peace. He told us: "If you want to help the third world, stay home and change your own society. Because the cause of our problems with poverty resides here in the North."

This prophetic word put me on the track of my new mission. I put it bluntly to myself: "You figured out how to adapt and fit in with people from other places, so do the same here. Adapt, and get to work!"

Contributing to the student movement

The MECQ (Quebec Christian Student Movement) was looking for a national chaplain who could help the organization to begin chapters in Quebec CEGEPs and universities. They invited me to work with them. I worked with the province-wide organization over a number of years, devoting my energies to organize students to encourage them to take control of their lives. See, judge, act! The neoliberals were advocating unfreezing tuition fees; according to them, education is a commodity and those who consume it must pay their share. We had to react! The state of political depression in Quebec had left the student movement in ruins, if not practically dead. It was painstaking work, filled with disappointments and failures, but also opportunities for political education and consciousness raising. With the Young Christian Students (YCS) active in the high schools, we worked to train Christian activists to become agents of change. My friend Jean Ménard, who had done solidarity work with trade unions and grassroots organizations, offered to consolidate the forces of MECQ in the Centre-Sud district of Montreal, where a dozen activists had recently moved. The years I roomed with Jean, two female students and a male student were for me a very important step, which allowed me to better understand the reality of my newly adopted land. We formed a base community called "Au pied du courant," in honour of the Patriots of 1837, who were hanged at the prison of the same name in the neighbourhood where we shared our experiences and our faith.

I also worked with Jeunesse du Monde (World Youth), a movement for teenagers designed to raise their awareness of international solidarity and enabling them to engage in it. There were many chapters for French-speaking students across Canada. We decided to send a team on a mission to a small village near the Orinoco Delta, on the Venezuelan border. With the participation of the Sœurs des Saints-Cœurs of Joliette, two young people from the Quebec World Youth leadership and three nuns conducted a pastoral and solidarity service for ten years that we regularly supported and visited, accompanying Quebec youth who were travelling there to fulfill their internships.

I have always found in the Entraide Missionaire network sisters and brothers who shared my vision of the Church and the world. The Justice Committee of the Quebec section of the Canadian Religious Conference invited me to participate in their work; we visited the regions and served as a bridge between local faith communities and community and grassroots organizations. I discovered a great prophetic dynamism, especially among the nuns who had been steadfast in their service to the poor and among the youth. These women greatly inspired me; they are true prophets living among us. I discovered in these networks a place of fellowship that allowed me to hold on.

Becoming a caregiver

Life often takes mysterious twists and turns; since my return to Canada, I had begun regularly visiting my mother, who was gracefully aging in Trois-Rivières. Widowed at the age of sixty, she remained a cheerful and sociable woman, who overflowed with vitality. But I felt her sliding progressively into solitude and in 1995, at the age of eighty-five, she had a first health glitch. Her spine had been weakened by osteoporosis, and she had to wear an aluminum corset she called her "hitch." Seeing her decline rapidly, I had to intervene. "*Maman*, you can't stay alone in this state. You need to make a decision: do you want to come and live with me in Montreal? Do you want to live in a residence?"

Montreal was a "no"! She would really be alone without a social network. As far as going into a home, that was a "no" as well. She wanted to stay in her home.

"So do you want me to come live with you?"

"But what about your ministry?"

"There is a commandment of God that says to take care of your parents. We'll be roommates, like the students."

And so I spent eleven wonderful years alongside the person that everyone in Trois-Rivières called my "roomie." After three months, she had completely forgotten her "hitch" and resumed her routine. What fortune and grace to be able to establish an adult relationship with the woman who gave you life! What complicity and what joy we experienced day after day, gradually settling into our domestic existence. For me, I couldn't have received a better education about aging. My mother died a natural death at the age of ninety-six. It made me realize how the presence of loved ones is essential for us to serenely cross the bridge of old age.

When I arrived in Trois-Rivières, the Solidarity Committee of Trois-Rivières, founded in 1973 to mark the coup in Chile, invited me to join its ranks and offered me a job. This would enable me to continue my solidarity work with the people of the South alongside young activists within an organization that shared my values. The Committee is an organization committed to local and international solidarity, a place of fellowship and openness. It became my adopted family, where I could rub shoulders with both idealistic young people and the veterans of the social struggle.

The Arche de Jean Vanier, which organizes homes for people living with intellectual disabilities, invited me to work with their community as a spiritual advisor. My contact with these people who speak the language of the heart, these "little people" of our world who have so much joy, spontaneity and love to bring us, taught me to "be" rather than to do things. I realized that my presence in Trois-Rivières would allow me to internalize my commitment to the poor and wounded.

Plus, a new commitment was waiting for me at the Cooke Home: I was hired by this long-term residential nursing home to support people who, because of their condition, had to rely on the help of others to live. My first visits to the residence left me with the impression I was entering a place of suffering, but I actually discovered a world of great depth. Being a spiritual care worker had become my job. My task was to help people with advanced chronic diseases, severe disabilities, paralysis, or who had simply reached a grand old age, to live in serenity and joy in this last stage of their lives.

My experiences with the communities of the Arche and the Cooke residence reconciled me with what it means to be a human being, and revealed to me the beauty of all beings. The people whom once a week I assembled to celebrate life were usually smiling, laughing. Their resilience, their attachment to life and their determination moved me. The CHSLDs (Long-term Residential Care Centres) in Quebec are, without being perfect, places where people continue to live full lives. The experience at the Arche trained me and also prepared me to enter into communication with people who had Alzheimer's disease, with whom the only possible communication is that of love. Through this experience, I was introduced to personnel who were careful and humane in the care they gave, from whom we demand a lot and who approach their tasks with dedication and empathy.

So the rebel priest in the time of tyrants now unfolds his commitment with happiness and serenity in the service of his peers. There is still much to do, but it is reassuring to know that what's coming after us is not the flood. New generations are coming forward to create the conditions for a better world. The Arab Spring, where the youth were on the front lines demanding change; the student struggles in Quebec in 2012, which revealed a militant youth standing up to neoliberalism and saying "no" to the commodification of their educations; the Idle No More movement, which has galvanized the First Nations into action for their emancipation; this is how the Good News is announced. The arrival of Pope Francis, determined to enter into dialogue with the modern world in an attitude of compassion and openness, brings to our Church a fresh perspective and gives us breath. In his apostolic exhortation "The Joy of the Gospel," Francis said "no" to the new idolatry of money; he spoke of a "tyranny" of money, an "unjust social and economic system that is crystallized in unjust social structures."[2]

All this gives me hope that, yes, another world is possible.

2. Pope Francis, Apostolic Exhortation, *Evangelii Gaudium*, [online] http://w2.vatican.va/content/francesco/en/apost_exhortations/documents/papa-francesco_esortazione-ap_20131124_evangelii-gaudium.html.

24
Homecoming

Santiago, Chile, January 2007

There was still ice on the St. Lawrence and the island of Montreal, bleak and gray, emerged through the dirty snow. In the plane that was flying me home from Santiago, the night was long. Thoughtful and collected in a world of my own, half asleep, I savoured the strong emotions that I had just experienced during my month-long visit in Chile. I was still moved, I couldn't really process what had just happened to me.

Twenty-one years after leaving Santiago, I had the desire to see my companions and comrades who had somehow survived the dark years of the Pinochet dictatorship. "What has become of all my friends, whom I held so close to me, whom I lov'd so much?"[1] But in my personal phone book I only had two phone numbers. I called Juan Carlos, now a sociologist at a hospital in the capital. I had known him when he was fifteen, child of a working-class family who wanted to do battle with the dictatorship.

"Come and stay with us," he said. "You'll meet my wife and my little Sofia. She really wants to see her grandfather!"

---

1. "Poor Rutebeuf, *or* Complaint of Friendship." English version by Riccardo Venturi, accessed online at antiwarsongs.org.

I called Reinaldo, my companion in the struggle; he also invited me to come and stay with him, his wife and their two teenagers.

On a Sunday afternoon in January, under a scorching summer sun, a dozen people waited for me at the Santiago airport. Juan Carlos hosted us in his courtyard with everything on the grill along with salads, watermelon and red wine. The reunion feast happily begun. Late in the afternoon, Reinaldo whispered in my ear: "It's time to go, the people of La Bandera wish to greet you."

For six years, during the most intense period of my stay in Chile, I had lived in La Bandera. Who would I meet there tonight?

Reinaldo smiled silently; a surprise was waiting for me. Seventy people were seated in a circle in a room at the Lutheran community centre. I was overwhelmed with emotion; I hadn't heard any news of them since 1980, and now, here they were in front of me with their children and their grandchildren. I had known them as adolescents or young adults, under a military dictatorship, out of work, out of money, hungry and victims of the daily violence of the police and the army, which had come down with full force on this "red" district.

There were members of our base community from the 1980s, leftists, comrades who had fought against the dictatorship. Dario, a political prisoner for fifteen years, had just been released; he was happy to be able to share this special moment. He too was meeting everybody for the first time in a long time. I've never been asked so many questions at once:

"Do you remember comrade so-and-so?"

"Do you remember when we ...?"

I could clearly recall some of the events, but was totally in the dark about others. Comments were flying in every direction: praise, jokes, anecdotes and more. I had the impression I was watching my own canonization, but without a devil's advocate to state the case against.

"My friends, you are very, very kind, and I am deeply moved to see you again after all these years. I would never have expected to meet so many people from the neighbourhood, my neighbours, my brothers and sisters from the community and the old guard of the resistance still fighting! When I arrived in La Bandera in 1977, I was a young priest and I moved into a neighbourhood hard hit by the disappearances, abductions, detentions and torture. Everywhere terror ruled, relentless. I didn't know what I was getting into, but you opened your hearts and your doors, you taught me about social struggle.

"I was initiated to the struggle by Rachel, "old Raca," a MIR activist who, despite a life of hardship, never gave up. She took me to my first demonstration, when the people began to reorganize. It was March 8, 1977, International Women's Day. When we got off the bus near Santa Laura stadium where the demonstration was being held, the army was waiting for us with armoured cars and special forces, ready to strike. I was scared to death, and Raca told me, 'Father, you want to be with the people, so come on!' We were unable to regroup and the military forced us out of the area with their batons. Raca began to harass a captain perched on a tank. Then I heard a revolutionary speech, seasoned with Chilean swear words.

"'So I guess you don't have a mother, mf c*! We are poor women who have nothing to eat. Our husbands are unemployed, our sons are in jail, our grandchildren malnourished ... and you, brave soldiers, you get off on beating up women! What courage!'

"The captain stood and took it, crimson and furious. I took hold of Rachel's arm and tugged on her fearfully to try to get her to disengage. She smiled at me mischievously ... I must have been white as a ghost ... and she opened her handbag a crack: it was full of good sized stones. This woman was not afraid of anyone! After a brisk dash out of immediate danger, we took refuge with a group of protesters in the cathedral. We barricaded the front door and we stayed locked inside for two hours, opening the doors for moments at a time to shout slogans when the soldiers moved away, abruptly slamming them shut when they reappeared.

"'Bread! Justice! Labour and Freedom!' Without intending to, I had just participated in the occupation of the cathedral.

"I told the women I was accompanying: 'You know, my mother thinks I'm trying to teach catechism in Chile!'

"These years with you, my friends, were among the richest of my life. It was very difficult, I admit; I had to question myself more than once, but you taught me what solidarity really is. I thank you. You are my family."

On a small table decorated with a plastic flower pot were placed a cup of wine and a loaf of Silvia's freshly-kneaded homemade bread. She invited me to share them as a sign of communion. I loved these people, and our feelings of closeness had obviously been maintained after a separation of many years, but it seemed to me that they idealized me too. A communist activist took the floor:

"Let me explain a few things, Claudio. During the dictatorship, you, the Quebec missionaries, worked in a number of working class neighbourhoods of Santiago. I lived with my family in the eastern zone; our wooden shack had a dirt floor and one winter evening, it flooded. We were covered by a couple of feet of mud and we lost everything. At midnight, in a driving rain, your brother René[2] arrived at our place, soaking wet, offering to help us. You never forget something like that! You loved us, you helped us, you shared our lives and you defended us during the most difficult years of our existence. That's why the people love you so much, and that's why I'm here."

At the end of the evening, when everyone was leaving, Salvador, a sixteen-year-old told his mother: "*Mamá*, you told me that this meeting was important, but I couldn't have imagined just how important it would be."

The following Sunday, Gabriela invited the members of the base community to meet with her at the foot of the Andes for a day of sharing. About fifty of us gathered, old-timers who

2. René Lapointe, priest of the Diocese of Saguenay, spent forty-four years defending the Chilean workers.

hadn't met for ages, their children, grandchildren and friends. The atmosphere was joyful, and I realized that my visit was the occasion for the community to hold a reunion. After our picnic on the grass, Gaby summoned us to the edge of the wading pool where the children dried off. She asked for silence.

> "The hard life we have lived separated us. We tried to survive with starvation wages and we are drowning in debt. I raised my daughter and two sons by myself and sustained them; we have experienced hunger and destitution, but I never stopped fighting. I have educated my children in the resistance and in solidarity, I wanted to pass on the values that have guided my life. I have prepared them all these years and I have been waiting for you so they could be baptized. Claude, I want you to communicate to them the same breath you gave us."

That day, on Gabriela's initiative, four adults and two children were baptized. The community found a new breath. Miriam, my old neighbour, then a little girl, who had become a social worker, spoke.

> "You know, we have been abandoned by the Church. André, Reinaldo and you, you were our neighbours. My father was unemployed, my mother worked as a servant in a rich family's house for starvation wages. We, the children, ate at the community kitchens. Your door was always open to everyone. After you left, other priests came to live in your house. They began by building a six-foot high brick wall and an iron gate to protect them from people. Their message was clear: we don't want to be bothered. Now, they've built a large church in the neighbourhood, without consulting anyone. The priest lives downtown and comes to say Mass on Sundays. They even refused us a hall to welcome you. That's why we turned to the Lutheran Church."

The plane touched the ground, and the vibrations of the engine shook me awake. I landed in Montreal, confirmed and happy. I was ready to move on. What is truly lasting in our lives is not our work or our achievements, but the real relationships we forge with our peers. Yes, really, "Love never ends."

¡Gracias a la vida que me ha dado tanto![3]
Merci à la vie qui m'a tant donné !
Thanks to life for giving me so much!

3. From the song of Violeta Parra, "Gracias a la Vida."

Epilogue

Who can fight the beast?

What is called 'globalization' is generally little more than the expansion of economic imperialism, which now dominates the planet. No people or nation can escape the logic of neoliberal capitalism; the big banks and multinational corporations now govern us all. Both those elected in our "democracies" and tyrants of all ilk bow down to the diktats delivered by the stock exchanges and rating agencies, the new masters of the world. Idolatry of Money is the mortal sin of humanity. We have blindly handed over the future of life on earth to the financial empire. We recognize the power of Money over us like a divine power that the Book of Revelations describes as the "vile beast." We are subjected to its absolute power. Any criticism of neoliberal capitalism is suspected of being heretical and traitorous. "Who can fight the Beast?"[1]

What does announcing the Good News to the poor and freedom of the oppressed consist of today? How can the eyes of the blind be opened in a context in which most media are sources of disinformation and lies? How can we announce debt cancellation and restoration of justice at a time and in places where maximum profits and unbridled wealth rule? That is the mission that believers have to take on in our societies where everybody is branded with the Beast's bar code.

---

1. *Book of Revelations*, 13, 1-11.

A Church focused on the Gospel

As a community of disciples, Jesus gave us a mission to go throughout the world to announce the Good News to the poor. Very early, however, (since emperor Constantine), the Church allied itself with imperial power and became itself a powerful institution. It now has to break with sixteen centuries of being in the bad company of political powers and return to its mission to serve the liberation of the poor. The Church is experiencing a profound crisis in our secular societies where it has little influence and finds itself subjected to an intense process of secularization. Its word is too often dogmatic, moralizing, and rigid; no one listens to it. The time of the "Christianity" that John Paul II and Benedict XVI dreamed of restoring is over, definitively. We have been returned to a Church of the Catacombs, on the margins, confronted like the poor and dispossessed disciples of the first centuries who dreamed of a world of equality, fraternity, and liberty.

In Quebec, the breadth and speed with which the Catholic Church has collapsed is spectacular. Religious communities that were so productive over the centuries are now disappearing in the infirmaries of homes for seniors. The clergy who were the key to Catholicism are now an endangered species. The sale and demolition of places of worship bear witness: we are at the end of a cycle. This should not be cause for gloom. These changes can be seen as the Breath of Jesus calling us to refocus our mission.

We now have the joy of having at the pinnacle of the Catholic family a man, Francis, a man of dialogue and openness, who is orienting us towards becoming a Church of the poor and the excluded. In the ponderous bureaucracy of the Vatican, so remote from the Gospel of Jesus, with its luxury and sacralised autocratic power, Francis has opened the door to reforms and asked us to focus on the Gospel. He should not be left to do it alone. We should follow his example and break with our routine rituals, weak-kneed spiritual comfort, and faith removed from reality, and face the challenges that our mission entails.

Seeking wisdom

It is time to stop asking the old sacred texts for ready-made solutions to today's challenges. Instead, together with our contemporaries and by trial and error, we must seek the wisdom that will guide us. It is our job to promote the respect of human rights everywhere, even in our Church, with respect to discrimination against women, homosexuals, and remarried divorcees. The Bible includes many profane passages with ancient wisdom that we consider to be the Word of God. God speaks to us in the wisdom of peoples. Solidarity should be our response. Within our sciences, laws, varied cultures, religious and spiritual traditions, social movements and all forms of humanism can be found the wisdom required to meet the great challenges of the day.

These challenges are urgent and they concern the future of life on earth:

- Combat the social inequalities that mushroom under the neoliberal dictatorship, and eliminate poverty on all the continents;
- Save the planet that is subjected to unbearable stress because of the economic pillaging, systematic destruction, and soon irreversible global warming;
- End the arms trade and the galloping militarization that feed ever more armed conflicts;
- Promote both collective and individual human rights everywhere;
- Encourage fraternal relationships among the different denominations and religions so that they will contribute, through their spiritual traditions, to peace and justice;
- Create human communities that are fraternal and in solidarity and take part in making the world more human, just and comradely.

Undertake to transform the world

In 2003, I was a member of the delegation of Canadian Churches to the World Social Forum in Porto Alegre, Brazil. On the first day, some one hundred and fifty thousand activists from throughout the world demonstrated against neo-liberalism and the U.S.-led invasion of Iraq. These rainbow multitudes of all political stripes and social backgrounds shared an experience of great intensity during the long march that culminated with a speech by Lula,[2] the newly elected president of Brazil. He spoke to us about hunger, poverty, and social justice. He made us dream. Shoulder-to-shoulder with these young and enthusiastic throngs, together lifted up by his words of hope, I cried with joy. "Yes," I thought, "here are the men and women who believe that a new world is possible and who march and work to make it happen. They are my spiritual family, my sisters and brothers, with whom I am in communion."

Until now, people entered the Church without having to choose an option. We inherited an ancestral faith with no specific commitment; baptism was automatic. Those times when faith would be simply transmitted from one generation to another are over. Becoming a disciple of Jesus of Nazareth is from now on, as it was at the dawn of the Apostolic Church, a decision, a commitment, a refusal to wear the bar code of the Beast, a break with a system of death, a real return. "Today, a Christian who is not revolutionary is no Christian."[3]

"I saw a new heaven and a new earth... these words are true."[4]

2. Luiz Inácio Lula da Silva, militant trade-unionist, first Brazilian president to come from the working class, elected in October 2002.
3. Pope Francis quoted in *Le Monde.fr* on 18 June 2013.
4. *Book of Revelations*, 21, 1 et 22, 6.

NONFICTION FROM BARAKA BOOKS

Justice Belied
The Unbalanced Scales of International Criminal Justice
John Philpot & Sébastien Chartrand, Editors

Slouching Towards Sirte
NATO's War on Libya and Africa
Maximilian C. Forte

Rwanda and the New Scramble for Africa
From Tragedy to Useful Imperial Fiction
Robin Philpot

Storming the Old Boys' Citadel
Two Pioneer Women Architects in Nineteenth Century North America
Carla Blank and Tania Martin

Challenging the Mississippi Firebombers
Memories of Mississippi 1964-65
Jim Dann

America's Gift
What the World Owes to the Americas and Their First Inhabitants
Käthe Roth & Denis Vaugeois

The Complete Muhammad Ali
Ishmael Reed

Journey to the Heart of the First Peoples Collections
Musée de la civilisation
Marie-Paul Robitaille, Director

The Question of Separatism
Quebec and the Struggle over Sovereignty
Jane Jacobs

Achevé d'imprimer
sur les presses de
Imprimerie H.L.N.
Imprimé au Canada - Printed in Canada